Anonymous

Progressive Hamilton.

A description of the village of Hamilton, New York; its scenery, material development, institutions of learning, and business enterprises

Anonymous

Progressive Hamilton.
A description of the village of Hamilton, New York; its scenery, material development, institutions of learning, and business enterprises

ISBN/EAN: 9783337713317

Printed in Europe, USA, Canada, Australia, Japan

Cover: Foto ©ninafisch / pixelio.de

More available books at **www.hansebooks.com**

PROGRESSIVE HAMILTON

A DESCRIPTION OF

THE VILLAGE OF HAMILTON

NEW YORK

Its Scenery, Material Development, Institutions of Learning,

and Business Enterprises

PRESS OF
HAWKINS & ELLIOTT.
HAMILTON, N. Y.

ENGRAVINGS BY
UTICA ENGRAVING CO.,
FROM PHOTOGRAPHS BY
H. H. HILL, HAMILTON, N. Y.,
ERNSBURGER, AUBURN, N. Y.

PROGRESSIVE HAMILTON

THE village of Hamilton, situated in the Chenango Valley, and surrounded by a picturesque landscape, is among the most progressive and promising villages of the Empire State. For years after the date of the Declaration of American Independence, the site of the now flourishing village was yet in the primeval forest. Not until 1812 did the struggling little hamlet assume the dignity of a "village." Thus a veritable wilderness on the outposts of civilization and overgrown with timber and underbrush, has, in a comparatively short period, been transformed, by the brain and hand of man, into a centre of human activity, with varied and growing interests, and with direct and rapid communication to all parts of the country. The insignificant hamlet, whose business consisted principally in a little barter in furs, grain and salt, has given way to one of the finest and most prosperous villages in the State, with spacious streets and imposing business blocks, handsome residences, and charming surroundings.

A BRIEF HISTORICAL SKETCH

Prior to 1792, Hamilton had no official existence, and until its incorporation as a village in 1812, it was known as Payne's Hollow. So far as can be learned, it contained but few white residents. The place was settled by Elisha Payne in 1792. He built a hotel on what is now the corner of Broad and Lebanon streets. Payne was married three times; his first wife, who died in 1796, was the first white person to die in Hamilton; she was buried in a plot of ground, (the present Lebanon Street Cemetery,) given to the settlement by Payne. The first Baptist Church was built in 1796, on the site now occupied by the north end of the Village Park. This building was destroyed by fire in 1801. The second edifice was erected on the lot north of the site of the burned Hotel Hamilton, and contained the first church bell ever hung in town. The main building was removed in 1845; the session room was transformed into the dwelling now on that lot. The third and present edifice was erected in 1843.

Br...Street L...N

Dr. Thomas Greely, Hamilton's first physician, settled here in 1796. The first grist mill was built in 1800, and was replaced by a new structure in 1808. This building is now standing near the railroad

M...Street L...N...

depot, and is the second oldest building in town. Two of the oldest buildings in Hamilton are those occupied by Frank Pierce and E. J. Enos. The first two stores were opened in 1806. One was located where the Fairchild residence stands on Broad street, and the other on the corner occupied by the Sperry building. The frame of the latter of these stores is now the frame of a Madison street barn. The Park House was built in 1807.

The first public hall was located in a hotel on Eaton street, built in 1811, and afterwards known as the Triangle Building. Hamilton Literary and Theological Institution, now Colgate University, was founded in 1818, and occupied the second story of a building on the

northwest corner of Broad and Pleasant streets. This building was destroyed by fire in 1855. Nichols and Beal's drug store was founded by Joseph Mott in 1822. The Congregational Church was founded in 1828, and Madison Street Cemetery was opened by that society in the same year.

The old Eagle Hotel was erected in 1830, and was the largest stone building between Utica and Binghamton.

The first fire company was organized in 1832. The work of constructing the Chenango Canal was commenced in 1833, and completed in 1836. The canal was discontinued in 1876. St. Thomas Church was founded in 1835. The Village Park on Broad street

Maple Street Looking West

was planted by Ferdinand Walker in 1835. The material for grading was taken from the Chenango Canal, then in course of construction.

Broad Street, Looking South

Hamilton Union School was opened in 1858.

St. Mary's Catholic Church was built in 1869, and destroyed by a tornado June 7th, 1875. The corner stone of the present church was laid in 1875.

The M. E. Church was moved to its present site in 1870. Previous to that it occupied the south west corner of Charles and John streets, but was originally built near Madison Reservoir.

The railroad was first opened from Utica to Hamilton in 1870.

Woodlawn Cemetery, which lies on the slope of the uplands west of the village, was opened in 1884.

Residence of Percival Wm. M. West

Its first officers were:

President,	W. R. BROOKS
Vice-President,	F. T. PIERCE
Sec. and Treas.,	M. TRIPP

TRUSTEES.

M. TRIPP,	B. F. BONNEY,	J. MASON,	E. W. FOOTE,
A. PIERCE,	W. R. BROOKS,	F. T. PIERCE,	J. M. BANNING.

EXECUTIVE COMMITTEE.

W. R. BROOKS,	M. TRIPP,	J. M. BANNING

SUPERINTENDENT.

C. F. STARR, acting

HAMILTON'S GREAT FIRE

Tuesday evening, February 19th, 1895, was bright and cold. About 9:10, P. M. the inhabitants of Hamilton were startled by the cry of fire. Little did they dream that the whole business portion of the town would be laid in ashes before morning. The fire started on Lebanon street in the furniture store of Messrs. Rowlands and Beal. Over twenty-five business blocks were burned, with a loss of between $300,000 and $400,000. The smoking ruins were a sad sight to the many village and country people, who came from miles around to look at them the next morning. Many said Hamilton was doomed; but with the enterprising spirit which the merchants had, they at

Shanty Town.

once began to erect temporary buildings in and around the Park. It was not many days before "Shanty Town" was running at full blast. Then the plans were made to rebuild the town better than before the fire. The present handsome business blocks fully tell the story. The many illustrations in this book testify to the fine appearance of Hamilton's business section of to-day.

AS A PLACE OF RESIDENCE AND OF BUSINESS

Hamilton offers many advantages. Its location is everything that can be desired, and its eligibility as a village of homes has been a prominent factor in the development of its natural resources. Its broad, well kept business thoroughfares, its handsome, tree-shaded residential streets, and its numerous elegant private residences, combine to make it an attractive place in which to live. Surrounded by a rich and fertile agricultural section, the citizens have an abundance of fresh and cheap food products of every description. The rent of dwellings is reasonable, the cost of building low. There are few who do not labor in some useful occupation. The wealth is well distributed among the population; there are many well to do, but few really poor, and shabby or unsightly houses are few in the village. The inhabitants generally are energetic,

pushing, and progressive, and there are few other villages in the Empire State that present such a healthy, solid growth, socially and morally, while the strength of position attained in trade is a standing tribute to the prudence and foresight of the capitalists, merchants, and investors who are here engaged in business pursuits. The mercantile establishments are many. Every description of merchandise can be purchased here. The stores are well stocked and admirably equipped. A classified list of the business houses in successful operation is given herewith:

Baker and Grocer.

Rogers, J. Frank, Madison street.

Bank.

National Hamilton Bank.

Barbers.

Timian, Frank, Lebanon street ; Edkins, Charles, Smith Building.

Blacksmiths.

Carp & Son, Green street ; Hand, Peter, Utica street.

Booksellers and Stationers.

Grant, J. B., Smith Building ; Stock, A. H., Opera House Block.

Plenty Town.

Carriage and Wagon Repository.

Matterson, H. H., Maple avenue.

Clothing and Men's Furnishings.

Baum, Carl & Sons, Lebanon street ; Lewis, A. E. & Son, Smith Building ; Piotrow, V., Lebanon street.

Coal Dealers.

Lampher, C. W. & Co., near railway station.

Contractors and Builders.

Kennedy & McDonald, Maple ave.

Crockery, Wall Paper, &c.

Royce, L. M., Smith Building.

Dentists.

Bardeen, A. V. & Son, Opera House Block ; Gardiner, James L., Nichols & Beal Block ; Root, A. E., Payne street.

Druggists.

Hamlin & Co., Lebanon street ; Nichols & Beal, Nichols & Beal Block ; Root, Elmer C., Smith Building.

Dry Goods, Boots, Shoes, Carpets, &c.

Sperry, Burt P., Smith Building ; Sperry, Geo. E., Lebanon street

Florist.

Fairchild, D. M., Payne street.

Flour and Feed.

Miller & Nash, opp. railway station ; Wickwire, N. R., Maple ave.

Foundry and Machine Shop.

Wilcox, B. Frank, Madison street

Furniture and Undertaking.

Rowlands & Beal, Lebanon street

Grocers.

Kelloway & Kingsbury, Nichols & Beal Block ; Nichols & Beal,

Nichols & Beal Block ; Root, Elmer C., Smith Building ; Royce, J. M., Smith Building ; Sheldon, E. B., Sheldon Opera House Block ; Wilcox, M. W., Lebanon cor. Maple ave.

Hardware Stores, Plumbing, Etc.

Gulbran, Charles G., Phoenix Block ; Smith, V. N., Smith Building

Harness Makers.

Knelley, M. J., Lebanon street ; Nash, H. H., Lebanon cor. Milford.

Hop Dealers.

Leland & Tanner, near railway station ; Shores, J. J., Sheldon Opera House Block ; Shores, Fred, Sheldon Opera House Block.

Hotels.

Maxwell House, M. J. Maxwell, Prop ; Park House, W. G. Lippitt, Prop.

Insurance.

Fitch, S. A., Nichols & Beal Block ; Foster, D. H., Madison street ; St. John, W. A., Opera House Block.

Laundry.

Hamilton Steam Laundry, Wheeler & Sweeney, Props., Kendrick cor. Maple ave.

Lawyers.

Cushman, E. Watts, Nichols & Beal Block; Hartshorn, Wm. M., Hamilton street; Mason Joseph, Bank Building; Sheldon, Albert N., Pine, near Maple ave.; Sheldon, Albert S., Pine, near Maple ave; Stimson, B. J., Phoenix Block; Underhill, Charles W., Payne

Residence of E. P. Sisson.

street; Welch, James W., Opera House Block; Wellington, Garrett L., Bank Building.

Livery Stables.

Clark, Millard J., Eaton street; Felt, Walter W., rear Park House; Rogers, J. E., Maple ave.; Tibbitts, Asa, Maple ave.

Lumber, Sash, Doors and Blinds.

Hamilton Lumber Co., near railway station.

Machinist.

Graham, Dwight, near railway depot.

Marble and Granite Dealers.

Van Vleck & Baker, Lebanon street.

Meat Markets.

Betts, Wm., Lebanon street ; Mooney, Michael, Lebanon cor. Maple ave ; Rogers, J. L., Lebanon cor. Maple ave ; Roth, Wm., Madison street.

Milk Station.

Harmon, John, near railway station.

Millinery and Fancy Goods.

Grosvenor, M. E., Mrs.

Musical Instruments.

Hall, A. L. L., Opera House Block.

Painter.

Keyes, Edward F., Maple ave.

Photographer.

Hill, Henry H., Opera House Block.

Physicians and Surgeons.

Bardwell, F. A., Broad street ; Gardiner, H. S., Broad cor. John ; Gifford, Gilbert L., Broad cor. Pleasant ; Langworthy, O. S., Payne street ; Lloyd, F. O., Broad street.

Plumbers and Gas Fitters.

Cleveland & Lennox, Lebanon street ; Smith, A. N., Smith Building.

Residence of L. W. Medbury.

Printers and Publishers.

Hawkins & Elliott, Publishers of the Hamilton Republican.

Real Estate.

Smith Bros., Smith Building.

Shoemakers.

McGraw, Hiram W., Eaton, cor. Montgomery ; Paterson, Robert, Lebanon street ; White, Peter C., Green street ; Williams, Wm., Maple ave.

Variety Goods.

Abel, Mrs. J. G. & Co., Smith Building.

Wagon Makers.

Abbott, Wm. H., Maple ave.; Richardson, LaMott, Eaton street

Watches and Jewelry.

Blumm, George F., Lebanon street; Sanford, Charles B., Lebanon street; Tompkins, F. N., Smith Building.

VILLAGE GOVERNMENT

Without efficient, economical local government, no community can be progressive or prosperous. The people of Hamilton, at an early period in their history, realized this fact. While at all times careful to preserve a low rate of taxation, the citizens have never been nig-

gardly in carrying out public improvements, and these have always been made in a way to ensure perfection and durability. As a consequence, the sanitary condition of the village has been maintained at a high standard, and this, coupled with the advantages of favorable location, has contributed to a low rate of mortality. Indeed, the mortality returns show Hamilton to be one of the most healthful villages in the state. The village has practically less than $25,000 indebtedness, and this, with its many improvements, water works, electric light plant, &c., gives a financial status that but few other villages in the country can equal. The property valuation is about $750,000, and on a fair estimate the real value is about double that amount. The taxation rate is $7\frac{60}{100}$ per $1,000 of assessed valuation. E. P. Sisson is President of the village.

The trustees are:

P. C. BROWNELL,	E. L. KINGSBURY,	S. D. SMITH.
H. H. MATTERSON,	C. R. PAYNE,	G. G. SPERRY.
Secretary,		B. J. STIMSON.

WATER WORKS AND ELECTRIC LIGHTS

The supply of water for household and manufacturing purposes, is practically unlimited, and protection from fire is as completely assured as in any village in the country. The water supply for Hamil-

Water Works and Electric Lighting Plant

ton is secured from Woodman's Pond. By gravity the water is carried a distance of two miles, through tile pipes, to the filter bed, and thence into the well; from there it is pumped into the tower or stand pipe having a capacity of 200,000 gallons, and sufficient elevation to give 100 pounds pressure per square inch into the pipe system. Citizens of Hamilton may well congratulate themselves, not only on the abundance of water with which the village is blessed, but on its excellent quality. The water works plant is owned and controlled by the village. Pure, wholesome water is therefore furnished to all, at a cost much less than that charged where the water works are owned by private corporations. The electric light plant is also owned and controlled by the village of Hamilton, and as to cost, the same remarks apply as to the water works. The electric light plant is one of the most complete in the State. Among the equipments, mention is made of two dynamos, one for arc light for street lighting, and the other for lights for incandescent for commercial purposes. The company furnishes a duplicate set of boilers and engines, so that down to any part of the machinery and trouble at the water works plant, there is a full complement of equipment in reserve to operate both plants. The contract for the equipment of the water plant was let to the Stilwell-Bierce Company, Kew

N. Y., who employed Mr. J. W. Clark of this village as the engineer in charge. The construction of the electric light plant was in of Mr. C. O. Mailloux, of New York city. The water works and electric light plants is under the of the following commissioners:

President,   W . M. W
Secretary,   James M. Taylor
Treasurer,   Melvin Fre

The present superintendent is F. L. King ay

FIRE DEPARTMENT

Hamilton possesses a good fire department w

trol of a chief engineer, and is composed of 70 men. The present fire department was organized in 1873, and is now about to be reorganized, in order to meet the present requirements arising from the new water system.

VILLAGE IMPROVEMENT ASSOCIATION

In order to promote the best interests of Hamilton, the Hamilton Village Improvement Association was organized June 24th, 1884. The organization began with about twenty members. The first work was to cut out trees from the Village Park, and to grade the same. This was done at an expense of $229, and from that time

forth the organization had the care of the Village Park. An extension south of this park has also been laid out at an expense of from $500 to $600, also a plot at the junction of Pine and Mill streets, and another on Lebanon street. With the exception of an appropriation of $20 per year from the village, they have borne the expense of the care of the park and plots. The association has expended several thousand dollars since its organization. Besides the direct improvements made by the association, much has been accomplished in the way of stimulating the individual property owners to more care and improvement of their private grounds. The Village Improvement Association has 31 members. Its present officers are as follows :

President, B. F. BONNEY
Vice-President, MELVIN TRH
Treasurer, LEROY FAIRCHILD
Secretary, E. P. ST ON

EXECUTIVE COMMITTEE.

E. B. GASKELL, L. M. ROYCE, J. M. ROWLANDS,
D. C. MOTT, WM. R. ROWLANDS.

FINANCIAL

Hamilton's banking business is perhaps the strongest support of the mercantile interests of the village. The National Hamilton Bank

is noted for its sound, energetic, yet conservative management. It commands the entire confidence of business men and capitalists, and holds a high rank among the financial institutions of the state.

TRANSPORTATION

The transportation facilities of Hamilton are furnished by the N. Y. O. & W. Ry., having direct communication with New York. Connections are made at Sidney with the D. & H. R. R., and at Utica with the D., L. & W. R. R., N. Y. C. R. R., and West Shore R. R.

PRESS

The press of Hamilton is fully up to the best grade of newspaper enterprise. The Hamilton Republican is issued weekly. It was established in 1830, and is now conducted by Hawkins and Elliott. The Madisonensis, a college paper issued from Colgate University, is also one of the leading publications of its class.

POST OFFICE

MAILS CLOSE.

NORTH. 6:55 A. M., 10:25 A. M., 5:00 P. M.
SOUTH. 9:20 A. M., 2:10 P. M.

MAILS ARRIVE.

NORTH. 9:43 A. M., 2:30 P. M., 6:51 P. M.
SOUTH.—10:51 A. M., 5:32 P. M.

Office hours from 7 A. M. to 8 P. M., daily, except Sundays and holidays.

Rev. George Sharpe, Pastor M. E. Church.

CHURCHES

Hamilton has five churches, and the uniformly large attendance bespeaks the high moral and religious character of the people. The churches, with a brief historical sketch of each, are as follows:

First Baptist Church

The first religious meeting in the town of Hamilton was held in June, 1796. In November of that same year the First Baptist

Church was organized with seven constituent members. Meetings were held for several years in private dwellings or in school houses. In 1802 the church called Rev. Ashbel Hosmer, who became its first settled pastor. He was succeeded by the following pastors: Rev. Daniel Hascall, 1813; Rev. Daniel Eldridge, 1829; Rev. Aaron Perkins, 1835; Rev. Leonard Fletcher, 1840; Rev. Beriah N. Leach, 1842; Rev. Chesson P. Sheldon, 1845; Rev. Isaac Bevan, (1848); Rev. Aaron Perkins, (1852); Rev. Chesson P. Sheldon, (1854); Rev. Hezekiah Harvey, 1857; Rev. Walter R. Brooks, 1858; Rev. James M. Stifler, 1873; Rev. Stephen H. Stackpole,

(1882); Rev. William N. Clarke, 1887; Rev. Cornelius S. Savage, (1891).

In 1816 the church granted letters to a number of its members who organized the Baptist churches in Eaton and Lebanon. In 1819 the Second Baptist Church was organized in the eastern part of Hamilton by members dismissed for this purpose.

In 1807 was formed by the church, the missionary society which became, in 1825, the Baptist Missionary Convention of the State of New York. In 1817 the Baptist Education Society was formed by members of this church, although the society was not incorporated until 1819.

The church has erected three houses of worship — the first in 1810 which was the first house of worship erected in this part of the State; the second in 1819, and the present building in 1843.

From the formation of the church, nearly one hundred years ago, to the present, there has not been a single Lord's day on which the church has not met for Christian worship. The present membership numbers 513.

St. Thomas' Episcopal Church

At a meeting held on September 21st, 1835, and presided over by the Rev. Mr. Barrows, of Sherburne, who was the first to hold Episcopal services in this village, a parish was organized under the name of St. Thomas' Church. Services were held for several years

St. Thomas' Episcopal Church.

in the Ladies' Academy, corner of Broad and Pleasant streets. On Sept. 4th, 1846, the corner stone of the present church was laid, a lot having been bought on Madison street a year or two previously. The church was finished in 1847, and consecrated on June 8th of that year, by the Rt. Rev. William Heathcote De Lancey, Bishop of Western New York, in which diocese this section of the State was at that time included.

The church property consists of an extensive lot on the east side of Madison street. The present buildings are the church, the rectory, and the parish building (the latter built in 1853, and long used for a parish school house,) with ample room for the enlargement of the present buildings, or the erection of new ones. The property is free from debt.

The parish organizations are the Ladies' Aid Society, or Senior Branch of the Woman's Auxiliary, and the Girls' Guild, or Junior Branch of the Woman's Auxiliary.

The church is a Gothic structure, furnished in a churchly manner, the altar, lectern, font, and several windows being memorials of former faithful members.

The parish numbers about 90 communicants.

Among the rectors who have been in charge of St. Thomas' parish, may be mentioned: Dr. Tyler, Dr. Porter, Dr. Murray, Dr. Wilkinson, Mr. DeMille, and Dr. Cross. The present rector is Frank P. Harrington, who came to Hamilton Jan. 1st, 1893.

The Congregational Church

The Congregational Church of Hamilton, and the religious society connected with it, were organized in 1828, and the first house of

worship was erected upon the present site the same year, although not dedicated until two years later. In 1832 the church was received into the fellowship of the Congregational order of churches, and the same year a Foreign and Domestic Missionary Society was established. From its early days the sentiment of the church was strongly anti-slavery, and it has been a promoter of temperance reform from the time of its foundation.

In 1851 the church building was totally destroyed by fire, but it was soon rebuilt, the present structure being dedicated in 1853. This building was improved and refurnished in 1871, at an expense exceeding the original cost of construction. A severe storm in June, 1874, overturned the spire, and otherwise damaged the church, but the injury was immediately repaired.

The original membership of nine communicants has multiplied until there are now 168 members. The Bible School enrolls 125 teachers and pupils. There is a Y. P. S. C. E. of 45 members, and there are 30 Junior Christian Endeavorers.

Beautifully situated just between the business and residence portions of the town, on the finest part of Broad street, opposite the Park, the church is easily accessible from the private residences and all the hotels. At a short distance from the church, on John street, is the manse belonging to the church where resides the pastor, Rev. Lathrop C. Grant.

St. Mary's Catholic Church.

St. Mary's Church

St. Mary's Catholic Church stands at the north end of the village on the corner of Utica and Wylie streets. It is a handsome stone structure of Gothic design. The architect was Isaac Perry, of Binghamton.

St. Mary's Catholic parish was organized by the very Rev. A. P. Ludden, V. F., now of Little Falls, in 1869. Previous to this the place was attended, from time to time, by priests from Norwich. Divine services were held for a time in the Town Hall, now the residence of D. H. Foster.

On the 28th of July, 1869, Lyman Rogers and wife deeded to Wm. McDonnell and John Kelly the first piece of land ever sold in

the village for a Catholic church; at different times up to April, 1878, other pieces were added, the total purchase being $1,105. A frame structure was erected on the ground, but a few years afterward was blown down in a violent storm one Sunday in June, shortly after the congregation had left. In 1875 Father Ludden laid the corner stone of the present building, which has the strength of a fortress. It cost about $20,000, and was generously subscribed to by many members of the other churches in town. Father Ludden also purchased, on April 1st, 1873, from Sandford Gardiner, five acres of land at $1,000, for the present handsome cemetery.

In September, 1880, Father Ludden was changed to Little Falls by Bishop McNeirney, and was succeeded by Rev. W. B. Hannett, of Amsterdam, who administered the parish till his death on the 17th of October, 1889. Father Hannett built the pretty Catholic church at West Eaton, which is attended from St. Mary's. The present pastor, Rev. J. V. MacDonnell, was appointed assistant to Father Hannett in July, 1888, and pastor in January, 1890, the outmission of Sherburne being cut off and created an independent parish.

The Late Father Hannett.

Father MacDonnell has succeeded in paying off, since 1890, debts to about the amount of $3,600, including $1,500 of the mortgage, the present mortgage being $4,500, held by the Dissel estate in Syracuse.

The present parochial house is what was the former frame church. The present value of the whole church property, including the cemetery, is $20,000. The trustees of this parish, as in every other parish in the Diocese of Syracuse, to which this Parish belongs, are the Right Rev. Bishop, the Vicar General, the pastor, and two laymen, who are nominated by the pastor.

The Bishop of the Diocese of Syracuse the Right Rev. P. A. Ludden, D. D., consecrated May 1st, 1887, and son-in-law to the Ver. P. A. P. Ludden, formerly pastor of St. Mary.

The number of Catholic families is about 60 and members about 320.

First M. E. Church

The history of the First Methodist Episcopal Church of Hamilton has been a history of persistent endeavor to sustain Methodist purposes and ends of Methodism in the community thereto.

Numerically the members hope has been small, but spiritually it has never failed, and its history has been felt in the community.

For many years previous to the present edifice a small chapel, which stood on the corner of East and Broad street, east from the village nearly two miles.

The present edifice was erected and has been occupied for more than 30 years, and was dedicated in the year 1867.

At no time has the property been exceptional in its character: the present parsonage, however, built last winter, is modern and complete in its appointments. (See page 19.)

The itinerant system has acted advantageously here. Ministers now high in the counsels of the church have served as pastors We scan the roll and read the names of such men as A. J. Crandall, (the first pastor,) Leonard Bowdish, S. P. Gray, W. R. Cobb, Dwight Williams, T. J. Bissell, Theron Cooper, W. S. Titus, I. D. Peaslee, G. G. Dains, Gordon Moore, E. W. Jones, Bishop E. G. Andrews, of New York, and Bishop J. P. Newman, of Omaha, Neb.

First M. E. Church.

The membership is now 133, and 20 probationers. Every department is carried on with zeal. Rev. George Sharpe is pastor.

EDUCATIONAL

As might be expected, from a flourishing and prosperous village, Hamilton has always been mindful of making adequate provision for her sons and daughters. The public school building is a substantial structure, and the newest and most approved methods of tuition are employed. It is known as the Union School and Academy, and is under the principalship of Prof. Chas. H. Van Tuyl, assisted by eight competent instructors, who keep the grade of the schools up to the highest standard. It is generally admitted that the work done in the Hamilton school, will compare favorably with that done in any other village in the State. The Board of Education is composed of the following gentlemen:

President, ADON N. SMITH.
Clerk, GEORGE BEAL.

TRUSTEES.

P. C. BROWNELL,	J. W. HURN,	O. S. NICHOLS,
N. R. WICKWIRE,	B. J. STIMSON,	U. C. VAN VLECK,
	R. W. THOMAS.	

A. N. SMITH

There is also "Emily Judson" Hall, a preparatory school for women, under the proprietorship of Mrs. Mary Davis Moore. This is an educational institution of much merit, and is highly endorsed by leading educators from this and other states.

Hamilton is also the seat of Colgate University, one of the lead-

ing institutions of higher learning allied with the Baptist denomination. The beautiful campus, of more than two hundred acres, lies just south of the village ; and the principal buildings rise on the slope of the hill overlooking the valley to the northward. The presence of the University has contributed much to the beauty and prosperity of the village, and has added to the other attractions of Hamilton all the advantages of a college town.

The institution was founded in 1818, as the Hamilton Literary and Theological Institution. In 1846 it was granted the full powers and privileges of a university, and assumed the name of Madison University. In 1890, its name was changed to Colgate University, in appreciation of the long continued and large beneficence of the Colgate family.

The University consists of three schools or departments under the control of one board of trustees. The oldest of these is the Divinity School, or Hamilton Theological Seminary. This occupies a beautiful building known as Eaton Hall, has a faculty of seven professors with additional instructors and lecturers, and has, usually, about fifty students. Next is the College, which has a faculty of twenty professors and instructors, and about one hundred and sixty students. Its buildings are as follows, in the order of their erection : West College and East College, used as dormitories ; Alumni Hall, used mainly for recitation purposes ; the Chemical Laboratory, the Library, and the Gymnasium. The preparatory school of the University is known as Colgate Academy. It occupies a well equipped building of its own, known as William Colgate Memorial Hall, and has, in addition, a smaller building called Taylor Hall, devoted to the uses of the Academy literary societies. It has a faculty of eight teachers, and about one hundred and twenty-five students.

The unproductive property of the University is worth in the neighborhood of $650,000. Its total productive endowment amounts to about $1,000,000. It is thus admirably equipped for the work of a first rate college, and its future prosperity is thereby assured, as also, in large measure, that of the village with which its history and life are so vitally connected.

FRATERNAL AND SOCIAL ORGANIZATIONS

The leading secret and beneficial societies are well represented. The lodges are generally well furnished, and great interest is taken in the organizations, as is testified by the constant growth of membership. The lodges are as follows :

Hamilton Lodge, No. 120, F. & A. M., has a membership of 106.

Its present officers are, Dr. George B. Palmer, Master ; Chas. H. Van Tuyl, Sr. Warden ; Wm. P. Sheldon, Jr. Warden ; Wm. M. West, Treasurer ; B. J. Stimson, Sec'y; John F. Howe, Tyler ; John J. Taylor, Sr. Deacon ; W. D. Stimson, Jr. Deacon ; Masters of Cere-

Store of Kell way & Kin... ure.

monies, A. P. Lewis and Geo. L. Waldron. Trustees, U. C. Van Vleck, F. H. Ingalls, Joseph Mason.

Cyrus Chapter, No. 50, R. A. M., has a membership of 91. The present officers are, Thos. H. Beal, High Priest ; Adon N. Smith, King ; H. S. Gardiner, Scribe ; U. C. Van Vleck, Treas. ; B. J.

Store — A. E. Lewis &

Stimson, Sec'y ; George L. Gifford, C. H. ; Chas. E. Smith, P. S.; Wm. P. Sheldon, R. A. C. ; John F. Howe, Sentinel ; Wm. Gavin, Sidney D. Smith, F. W. Piotrow, Masters of Veils. Trustees, V. Piotrow, Wm. M. West, E. E. Welton.

Odd Fellows, Tuscarora Lodge, No. 660, was organized in Oct., 1893, and has a membership of 94. The officers at present are, J. M. Welch, Noble Grand; Charles Barney, Vice Grand; L. F. Reed, Recording Secretary; G. H. Perkins, Permanent Secretary; J. W. Rowlands, Treas.

Waukesha Encampment Patriard. I, No. 101, has 23 members. The present officers are, M. J. Clark, C. P.; C. E. Richardson, J. W.; F. H. Crosby, Treas.; G. H. Perkins, Scribe.

Hasbe Lodge, No. 76, Daughters of Rebecca, has 56 members. The present officers are, Anna Murdock, N. G.; Jennie A. Campbell, V. G.; Fannie Perkins, Sec'y; J. L. Brown, Treas.

Hamilton Lodge No. 8, A. O. U. W., has 74 members. Its present officers are, Thomas Stradling, Past Master Workman; J. I. Baker, Master Workman; Perley Fiske, Foreman; N. Petrow, Overseer; J. Stone, Recorder; Martin McDonald, Financier; E. B. Sheldon, Receiver; G. G. Sperry, Guide; W. W. Rix, I. W.; Thos. Flaherty, O. W. Meeting nights 2nd and 4th Mondays, in Russell Hall.

Woman's Christian Temperance Union. The present officers are Mrs. A. E. B. Campbell, Pres't; Mrs. C. M. Hartshorn, V. P.; Miss Lucinda Blakeman, V. P.; Miss M. A. Hopkins, Cor. Sec'y; Mrs. R. W. Hulburd, Rec. Sec'y; Mrs. B. F. Thurston, Treas.

Residence of Mrs. Martha B. Smith.

Hamilton Grange, No. 648, P. of H. Its present officers are J. S. Kimberly, Master; L. S. Coe, Overseer; A. E. Coe, Sec'y; L. F. Reed, Treas.

Hamilton Lodge, No. 599, I. O. G. T., has 40 members. L. D. Johnson, Chief Templar.

Residence of Elam P. A. Chesebrough

Hamilton Union, No. 476, E. A. U., has 136 members. Its present officers are, J. S. Kimberly, P.; Harriet Matterson, V. P.; Maud Reed, Advocate; Mary E. Grosvenor, Sec'y; Fidela Staples, Accountant; A. N. Enos, Treas.; J. F. Goodrich, Chaplain; Ellen Kelley, Au.; Fannie Perkins, Conductor; Hattie Kimberly, Warden; Mrs. Kelly, Sentinel; E. Keyes, Watchman.

Arthur L. Brooks Post, G. A. R., has 48 members. Its present officers are R. D. Spencer, Commander; J. W. Bryant, S. V. C.; A. M. Stevens, J. V. C.

Arthur L. Brooks Relief Corps, No. 7, has 30 members. Its present officers, are, Julia D. Beebe, Pres't; Mary Stevens, V. P.; Veronica Habbermann, J. V. P.; Betsy Thurston, Sec'y; Mary E. Grosvenor, Treas.

Mystic Order Veiled Prophets of the Enchanted Realm

The above organization was inaugurated by 17 members of Hamilton Lodge, No. 120, F. & A. M. The object was purely for a local social organization. The originators had no idea of its passing outside of the boundaries of Hamilton; but as visitors of other lodges received the degree, and were pleased with its work, and desired to open the order elsewhere, the originators decided to change the work and get up a Ritual worthy to go abroad. On June 13th, 1899, a meeting of the following members was held at Hamilton to organize a "Supreme Council," which should be the head or governing body of the world, and from which subordinate bodies (called Grottos) should receive their charters: George H. Raymond, (Grand Lecturer, Grand Lodge F. & A. M., State of N. Y.,) N. Y. City; Dr. J. B. Murray, (Grand Chaplain of the Grand Chapter R. A. M., State N. Y.,) LeRoy Fairchild, Thos. H. Beal, Adon N. Smith, B. J. Stimson, Prof. J. F. McGregory, Lieut. W. C. Eaton, C. M. Wickwire, J. W. Clark, R. R. Riddell, George Beal, Prof. B. S. Terry, S D. Smith, of Hamilton, N. Y. The Hon. George H. Raymond being elected chairman, the meeting proceeded to the adoption of a constitution and by-laws, and the election of the following officers: Hon. Thos. L. James, (ex-P. M. General,) N. Y. City, Most Potent Grand Monarch; Le Roy Fairchild, Hamilton, N. Y., Right Potent Deputy Grand Monarch; Hon. Geo. H. Raymond, New York City, Right Eminent

Residence of E. B. Gaskell.

Grand Chief Justice; J. C. Terry, 33°, St. Paul, Minn., Eminent Grand Master of Ceremonies; Prof. Oren Root, Clinton, N. Y., Eminent Grand Keeper of the Sagas; Rev. J. B. Murray, 32°, Auburn, N. Y., Eminent Grand Orator; Gen. Wm. M. West, Hamilton, N. Y., Eminent Grand Treasurer; Sidney D. Smith, Hamilton, N. Y., Eminent Grand Secretary; U. C. Van Vleck, Adon N. Smith, and D. B. West, Hamilton, N. Y., Eminent Grand Trustees; Prof. J. F. McGregory, Hamilton, N. Y., Eminent Grand Alchemist; B. J. Stimson, Hamilton, N. Y., Eminent Grand Master of Ceremonies; J. W. Clark, Hamilton, N. Y., Eminent Grand Steward; Thos. H. Beal, Hamilton, N. Y., Eminent Grand Captain of Guard

The ritual of the order was evolved from the various ideas suggested by the fun-loving spirit that inspired the original seventeen,

and in this respect to Hamilton are entitled to consideration as best has shown that patience easily... Mr. R. R. R......... Mr. R. S. S. .... Mr. G.........

Residence of Mrs. Dr. F. D. Beebe.

of their work is largely due to the literary abilty and keen love of fun for which Mr. Riddell is distinguished ; he entered into the spirit of the work, and gave it that peculiar charm and brilliancy which has won for the order the highest compliments from men of education and ability. While none but master masons are eligible to member-

Residence of Mrs. A. B. Campbell.

ship, yet the degree is in no sense a masonic degree. There are now nine Grottos established in this State, among which are prominent:

Azim Grotto, at New York city; Adon Smith, Monarch.

Lalla Rookh Grotto, at Rochester, N. Y.; George F. Loder, Past Grand Commander K. T., State of N. Y., Monarch.

Zuleika Grotto, Buffalo; Louis P. Adolff, Jr., Monarch.

Mokanna Grotto, Hamilton, N. Y., the Mother Grotto; Le Roy Fairchild, Monarch.

There is a Grotto established in Minnesota, and an application has just been received for a charter for a Grotto at San Francisco, Cal. Among the prominent members of the order, are Hon. Thos. L. James, ex-P. M. General; Thos. H. Caswell, of San Francisco, Cal., Grand Commander Supreme Council 33°, A. A. S. R., Southern jurisdiction; Col. S. M. Todd, of New Orleans, La., Grand Auditor Supreme Council, 33°, A. A. S. R., Southern jurisdiction

Dr. James Byron Murray, Grand Chaplain Grand Chapter, R. A. M. State of New York; Prof. Oren Root, of Hamilton College; J. C. Terry, 33°, St. Paul, Minn.; Adon Smith, 32°, Foreman Short Jury, New York city; Bishop Newman, and others.

At the annual meeting of the Supreme Council, held in the city New York in June, 1895, a new constitution was adopted, and a resolution passed not to grant a charter hereafter to any city of less than 50,000 inhabitants. The following officers were elected: A. Smith, New York City, Grand Monarch; Le Roy Fairchild, Hamilton, N. Y., Deputy Grand Monarch; Geo. F. Loder, Rochester, N. Y., Grand Chief Justice; J. Harris Bolston, Brooklyn, N. Y., Grand Master of Ceremonies; Gen'l Wm. M. West, Hargreaves, N. Y., Grand Treasurer; S. D. Smith, Hamilton, N. Y., Grand Secretary; W. H. Whiting, Rochester, N. Y., Grand Keeper Archives; Prof. J. J. McGregory, Hamilton, N. Y., Grand Orator; Obadiah Appleton, Louis P. Adolff, Jr., Buffalo, N. Y., Grand Captain Guard; A. N. Smith, Hamilton, N. Y., Grand Standard Bearer; Geo. B.

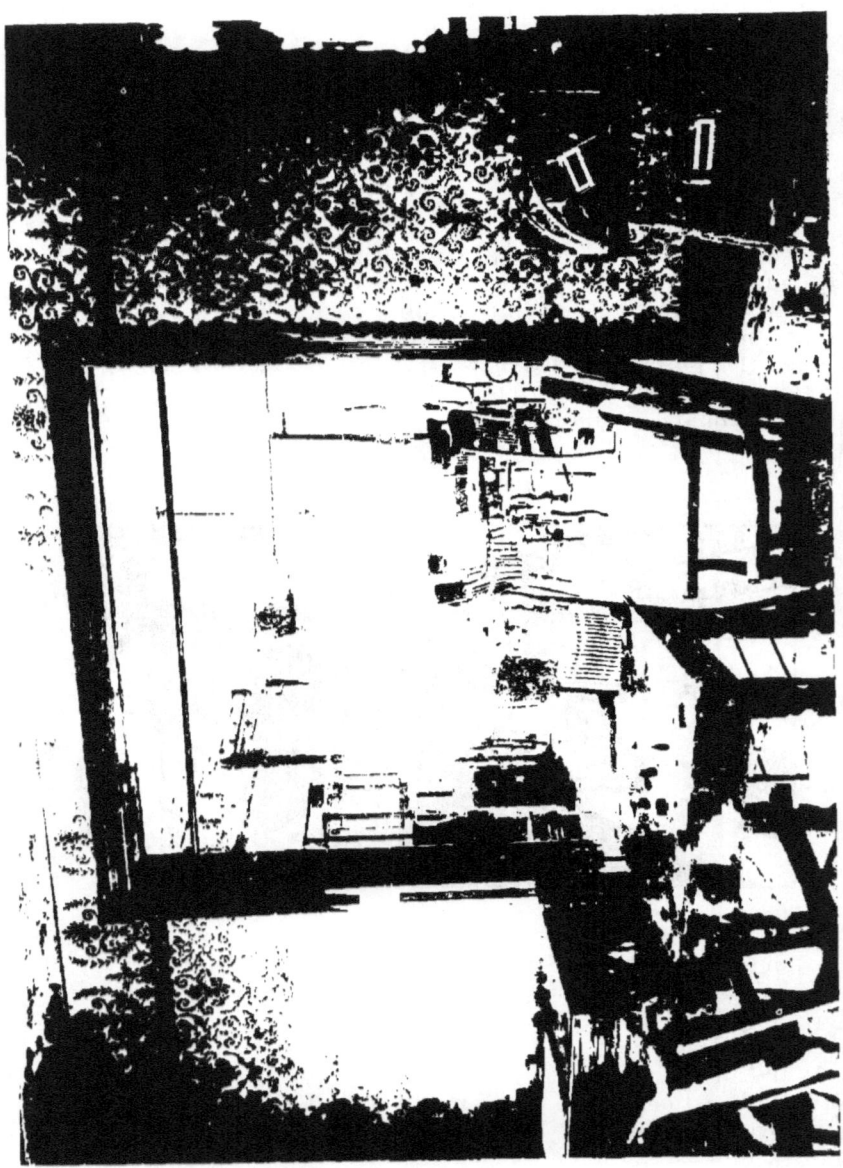

CITIZENS' CLUB

Hamilton, N. Y., Grand Marshal; Prof. Oren Root, Clinton, N. Y. Grand Alchemist; H. H. Brockway, N. Y. City, Grand Steward

Hamilton Social Club. Organized in 1876, has a present membership of 25. Its present officers are, F. M. Elliott, President; Thos. H. Beal, Vice President; W. J. Banning, Sec'y and Treas. Governors: J. W. Clark, A. P. Lewis, O. S. Nichols.

The Citizens' Club of Hamilton was organized Nov. 18th, 1895, and incorporated Dec. 26th, 1895, and has a membership of 33. Present officers: Dr. F. O. Lloyd, President; C. H. Van Tuyl, Vice President; A. N. Smith, Treasurer; Geo. Beal, Secretary.

AMUSEMENTS

The Sheldon Opera House was erected during the past year, and is, in every respect, a credit to this community. The best entertainments that can be secured are brought here. Aside from regular theatrical performances, the Sheldon Opera House is also let for lectures, entertainments, social gatherings, &c. The house is in every way first-class, and is one in which the citizens of Hamilton take much pride.

Besides the opera house there are also halls, and some form of entertainment is going on almost nightly in the winter season. Indeed, there is no lack of amusements in Hamilton.

HOTELS

The circumstance that so many traveling men make it a point to stay over in Hamilton, speaks volumes for the hotels. The Park House is one of the historic features of the town. This house was erected in 1860. The building has been remodeled from time to time, and is a comfortable stopping place.

The Maxwell House was erected during the past year. It is a modern hotel built of brick, is three stories high, and is supplied with all the modern improvements. So far as hotels go, Hamilton need not go to the rear for any place of twice its population.

In the following pages will be found a detailed and interesting description of the principal institutions and commercial concerns of Hamilton.

COLGATE UNIVERSITY

The history of the institution that is now called Colgate University may best be divided into three parts, corresponding to the three names that it has borne in successive periods.

Hamilton Literary and Theological Institution

The Baptist Education Society of the State of New York was formed September 24th, 1817, by thirteen men, who met and prayed together for the cause that was near to their hearts, and laid down a contribution of a dollar apiece for the new foundation. The society was founded to aid in the education of ministers. It did not in its formation pledge itself to the establishment of a separate school of its own, but the logic of the situation quickly led to such action, and plans for a school were soon undertaken. Daniel Hascall was the first teacher, Nathaniel Kendrick was the second; Jonathan Wade was the first student, and Eugenio Kincaid was the second, both of them known and honored through long lives as foreign missionaries of great power. Hamilton was selected as the home of the new institution, not without comparison with other places. Instruction was for a short time private and informal, but on May 1st, 1820, the school was formally opened under the name of "The Hamilton Literary and Theological Institution," in a building already used for educational purposes in the village of Hamilton, where Mr. E. W. Cushman's house now stands. The first building for its exclusive use, long since demolished, was erected on the plain in 1823. In 1826, Samuel Payne and his wife presented to the Education Society their farm, including the "hill" which has since become historic. On the new site the second and third buildings, still standing and in use, were erected in 1827 and 1834.

The course of study began with three years, but this was soon found insufficient, and the period was extended to four years in 1829, to six years in 1832, and to eight years in 1834. From this last date the course compared favorably with that of most colleges and theological seminaries of the time, and the graduates were virtually collegiate graduates, though the institution had no authority to grant them degrees. All students at first were students for the ministry, and this continued until 1839; at that date the school was opened to other students. A strong faculty was gradually formed, including men who have since been eminent elsewhere, and work far in advance of the time was done in the Biblical department. The interior life of the institution was intense and profitable. The work of foreign missions was new in those days, and a large number of the graduates entered upon it. Besides, there were men in considerable number who gave themselves to missionary work among the North American Indians, which was then a work of great difficulty and hardship. At the same time the contribution of Hamilton to the working body of the pastorate at home, was large and substantial. Any one who has had knowledge of the Baptist denominatoin in the United States during the last half-century, knows how greatly it is indebted to the Hamilton of the early days for its actual working force

Madison University

With the growth of the institution and the development of its course of study to collegiate proportions, came naturally the desire for a regular collegiate organization. In 1840, and again in 1843, the Education Society sought incorporation for its board as a college board, with full powers under the law; but the society was not so constituted as to meet the requirements of the State in such a case, and the applications were unsuccessful. In 1846, however, the Edutation Society adapted its request to the necessity, and petitioned for the establishment of a new corporation for collegiate purposes; and this application was successful. The new college was named "Madison University," an accidental name, for which no fitness was ever claimed, except that the institution stood in Madison county, counties being then much more prominent than now for purposes of local designation. Tradition reports that the name "Chenango University" was talked of, inasmuch as the location was at the head of the Chenango valley; but the legislature objected, on the ground that the place was not in Chenango county.

Dr. Nathaniel Kendrick had been acting as president for some years, though he had never consented to accept the office, and this arrangement continued till his death, in 1848, after which the office was vacant till 1851. Scarcely had the new era opened, when there arose a conflict that lasted three years with great bitterness, and left lasting consequences, upon the proposal to remove the whole institution to Rochester. The endeavor to remove it was not successful, as the contest developed legal obstacles to removal that could not be overcome. The institution was fastened in Hamilton; but in 1850 the larger part of the faculty withdrew and entered the service of the institutions that were founded in Rochester when the effort at removal had failed, and the most of the students went with them. A new faculty was gathered, however, short though the notice was, and the session of 1850-51 opened with a working force of instructors, and with thirty-three students. But the institution had a very deep and powerful hold upon the part of the denomination that stood by it, and within a few years the number of students was as large as before the trouble. In 1851 Dr. Stephen W. Taylor assumed the presidency, which he held till his death in 1856. He was succeeded by Dr. George W. Eaton, who had been connected with the institution since 1833, serving it faithfully in the various work that falls to the lot of a willing friend in the early life of a school. He held the presidency until 1868, and remained president of the theological seminary to his death, in 1872. In 1868 the presidency was assumed by Dr.

President Dodge.

Ebenezer Dodge, who had been a professor in the seminary since 1853. He conducted the affairs of the university for more than twenty-one years, until his death in 1890. The earlier history had been sorely embarrassed by the removal controversy, which almost destroyed the institution, and by the Civil war, in which the university contributed to the national cause one professor, one tutor, and about thirty students, and suffered, besides, as all schools suffered from the general depression. But in Dr. Dodge's administration times were more quiet, opportunities for progress were better, and larger gains were made.

No questions of endowment arose in the first period of the history as the institution was at first dependent directly upon the church, and many of its friends believed that its highest prosperity would be served by keeping it there. At the close of the removal controversy

the university was about $20,000 in debt. But friends were raised up, debts were gradually removed, and permanent funds came into existence, so that in 1871 there was reported as invested endowment of $290,090.86. When the second period closed and Madison University had existed twenty-five years, it had products of prosperity amounting $350,000.

For a long time students of every grade of preparatory, collegiate, theological, were mingled in one set of dormitories and classrooms, met in chapel together, and had common recitations. In early days there was a common boarding-hall for them all, and they all ing where Alumni Hall now stands, and then in a larger building on the plain reached by a walk through the wonderful beauty of the Eaton woods ; but even before fire destroyed the later structure, the life of the common table had begun to be broken up. The first great differentiation in the general life occurred in 1873, when the preparatory school, known till then as the grammar school of Madison University, was set off to work in a building of its own, under the name of "Colgate Academy." The building on the plain, with its grounds, was the gift of Mr. James B. Colgate, in memory of his father and mother, whose love and prayers for Hamilton were among the re-

Eaton Hall.

membrances of his childhood. Mr. Colgate and his partner, Mr. John B. Trevor, set apart a special sum as an endowment for the academy. The school has long held an honorable rank among the secondary schools of the State, and can look back upon an honorable history.

The next differentiation occurred in 1886, when the theological seminary withdrew from life in common with the college, and entered its own building, to which the name "Eaton Hall" has very properly been given. This building, standing on the beautiful site of Dr.

Eaton's former home, was erected by contributions from many friends, at a cost of about $65,000, and is one of the most convenient buildings for the use of a theological seminary that the country contains.

Other additions to the buildings were made within the second period. In 1860 there was erected, by subscription, at a cost of about $20,000, the unbeautiful but useful Alumni Hall. The president's house, which stood on land adjacent to the campus, was purchased in 1868. The chemical laboratory was erected by the generosity of a few friends, about 1885. The campus was largely extended by the purchase of land on the plain, between the hill and the village.

All through this period the university was slowly but steadily growing stronger, and the quality of its educational work was improving. Difficulties were many, especially by way of financial limitation, but with patient and watchful labor good results were obtained, and a good body of honorable and loyal alumni was sent out into the world. The ministry is still largely indebted to the university, but a steadily increasing number of men have gone into other professions and departments of the world's work, and the body of alumni has become diversified, as well as widely scattered. Not a few graduates send their sons back to the old place for education. Some one long ago applied to the institution the motto from Paul, "As poor, yet making many rich"; and there are many who can gratefully bear witness that the words are truthfully used of Madison University. In proportion to facilities, few schools have been so richly useful.

Colgate University

Twenty-six years were passed under the first name, and forty-four under the second. Within the first decade of the Hamilton Literary and Theological Institution, deacon William Colgate, of New York, became warmly interested in its work. He gave it his heart, and was constant in prayer and effort for its success. He and his family made constant contributions for its support, even in the early days, and during the dark time that followed in its later history, he was one of the most earnest and steadfast of its friends. At his death, which occurred in 1857, his two sons felt that the interests of the institution that he and their mother had loved, came to them as a sacred trust. They soon became members of the official boards, and entered upon a course of active helpfulness that has never since been interrupted for a day. In all respects, Mr. James B. Colgate has been the largest contributor to its funds that the university has ever known, and Mr. Samuel Colgate has been the steadfast and generous supporter of the Education Society, of which he has been the president for many years, and of the theological seminary. President Dodge came to feel the need of a more distinctive name for the university, the name "Madison" having never possessed anything more than an accidental appropriateness; and in view of this need, and of the long and invaluable services of the Colgate family, he proposed to substitute "Colgate" for "Madison" in the official name of the university. He died before the desire of his heart was gained, but the end was accomplished at last, and since the spring of 1890 Colgate University has been in existence.

Library Building.

When the change of name was effected, the new library building, the gift of Mr. James B. Colgate, was already in process of erection. It is now completed and in use, the library having been catalogued and arranged according to modern methods, when it was transferred to its new home. The building is the most prominent object in the landscape as one looks from the village toward the hill. Besides the library of the university, it contains the great collection that Mr. Samuel Colgate has for many years been making of Baptist documents — minutes, reports, catalogues, periodicals, biographies, sermons, and books and pamphlets of every kind on Baptist subjects. The building also contains the office of the treasurer, and various

rooms for various uses. The reading room is well stocked. The library is growing, not so rapidly as might be desired, but steadily, and is made easily available to students.

The latest building that has come into existence is the gymnasium, standing just at the foot of the hill. It was not built without due consideration, for the architect made careful study of his problem, and learned from the successes and failures that have appeared elsewhere. Larger institutions have larger gymnasiums, but it is doubtful whether any of them are more wisely planned or more thoroughly adapted to their purpose than the new gymnasium at Colgate. At the beginning of 1896 it was opened for use, with excellent equipment, and under the care of a competent director.

The Payne farm, with the land that has been acquired about it, offers a most delightful situation for a college, and the beauty of the hill is lovingly remembered by all students of all periods. Where on earth is there a lovelier group of foliage than is seen in the little wood that surrounds Eaton Hall? Until of late, however, nature has been left to provide attractions for the campus, with only occasional help from man, and that not always best devised. But a few years ago, Mr. E. W. Bowditch, of Boston, the eminent landscape gardener, was employed to make a systematic survey of the premises, and improvements are now being made in accordance with his very intelligent and tasteful plan. The greatest part of this work yet remains to be done, but some things have been done as Mr. Bowditch planned them, and the result commends the design, and makes us long for the completion. At every turn his well-trained eye has discerned the best thing to do, and the beautiful hill will be vastly more beautiful when once he has had his way with it. At the same time a complete system of sanitary drainage has been put in, at considerable cost, and all the buildings of college, seminary, and academy are now connected with a system of sewers which is amply sufficient to its purpose. The village water and light will soon be in full use. Land recently purchased on the east of the campus is intended to provide sites for a group of professors' houses, and one 'ouse has already been erected. On Broad street, near the Academy, the Taylor house, once a somewhat unsightly structure, has been transformed into a handsome colonial-looking house for the accommodation of the literary societies of the Academy.

By far the larger part of these improvements has come from the generous mind of the man who received the financial interests of the university as a trust from the earlier Colgate. But back of all improvements, enlargements, lies, of course, the question of endowment At commencement-time, in 1891, Mr. James B. Colgate announced a gift to the university of $1,000,000 in interest bearing securities, one-half to come into use almost immediately, and one-half to accumulate as a fund for future needs. This splendid gift, which was one of the noblest ever made for educational purposes in America, immediately gave to the university a new fame and standing among institutions of learning, and vastly enlarged its possibilities. The fund thus established was most worthily named the Dodge Memorial Fund; and the friends of the university could not but wish that the president, whose name it bears, might have lived to see so fine an addition to the resources and facilities of the institution to which he gave his life for many years.

In addition to this, the university has since received a bequest of somewhat over $75,000 from the estate of the late Eli Perry, of Albany, for the benefit of the department of homiletics in the theological seminary, and a gift of $20,000 from the Joslin family, of Troy, in memory of the late J. J. Joslin, for partial endowment of the department of Christian theology. From Mrs. George Harrison, of Troy, there has come a gift of $10,000 for the completion of Eaton Hall.

Colgate University at present is, popularly at least, the comprehensive name of a group of three schools. The college occupies the original site, and the original buildings, with what have been added to them. The theological seminary stands a little to the west, on nearly an equal elevation. The academy is half a mile northward, on the plain. The three schools are under one management. The corporation of Colgate University directly and wholly controls the college and the academy. Until recently the Education Society retained actual direction of the affairs of the theological seminary, though it acted under a compact with the university, whereby the administration was, in certain respects, shared by the two bodies. In 1893 the compact was reconstructed, and the actual direction of the affairs of the seminary was made over to the university. The Education Society retains, however, the right and duty of visiting the seminary, and reporting to the university upon its work, and still holds an influential part in the election of theological instructors.

The death of Dr. Dodge was followed by a long vacancy in the presidential office, during which Dr. N. Lloyd Andrews was the dean and acting head of the faculty. In July, 1895, the presidency was filled by the election of George William Smith, who, for three years, had been professor of history at Colgate.

The collegiate catalogue of 1895-96 contains the names of sixteen professors, all but one of them in active service, and five assistants. There are three courses of study, equal in extent, leading to the degrees of Bachelor of Arts, Bachelor of Philosophy, and Bachelor of Science. After 1896, the Master's degree will no longer be conferred

President George W. Smith.

in course, after the ancient method, but only upon examination. The departments of instruction in the college are Latin, Greek, Semitic languages, English literature, French and German, physics and astronomy, geology and natural history, chemistry and mineralogy history and economics, rhetoric and public speaking, history of art, philosophy, and pedagogy. There is a department of university extension, and for the last few years professors have been doing a considerable amount of work in lecture courses in various places, for the promotion of general education. The catalogue records 48 freshmen, 57 sophomores, 41 juniors and 21 seniors. The greater part come, of course, from the State of New York, but of the 167 on the list 45 come from beyond it. The students maintain six institutions among themselves as students delight in. There are five fraternities—the Delta Kappa Epsilon, the Delta Upsilon, the Beta Theta Pi, the Phi Kappa Psi, and the Phi Gamma Delta. Three of these have chapter houses of their own, and the other two possess rented houses, in which they have their boarding clubs and live together. The fraternity life is on the whole very well conducted, and as much of the good, and as little of the evil of such life is experienced here as anywhere. The students have their athletics, and take delight in them. There are pennants from the base-ball and foot-ball fields hung up in the library in memory of past glories, and the college still maintains a good standing in this department of effort.

Of Colgate Academy, Eugene P. Sisson is at present the acting principal. There are six full instructors, and four assistants, and there are 112 students, in four classes. The academy is well equipped in the library, gymnasium, and chemical and physical laboratories for work of academic grade.

The theological seminary has never changed its name, but is still known as the Hamilton Theological Seminary, though it is a department of Colgate University. Dr. Sylvester Burnham is the dean of the faculty. There are seven departments of instruction—Old Testament Interpretation, Semitic Languages, New Testament Interpretation, Church History, Christian Theology, Homiletics, and Pastoral Theology; but there are at present only six professors in actual service, the department of Pastoral Theology having been temporarily united to that of Homiletics. In 1895-96 there are 46 students, in three classes, of whom only 21 come from within the State of New York. There are three courses of study—the full course, the Greek course, and the English course—each covering three years. To Bachelors of Arts who complete the full course and fulfil certain requirements, the university gives the degree of Bachelor of Divinity. The seminary has a regular lectureship founded in memory of the late Dr. Walter R. Brooks, on the relation of science and religion, and another on pastoral experience, filled annually by some successful

ful minister. It also has lectures on sociology, and other subject. The students have full use of the Colgate library, and have a small reference library in their own building. The seminary was never before so well organized for work as at present. The introduction of the elective system a few years ago proved highly beneficial, and no one would now return from it to the former method.

Journalism has not been neglected in the university. The collegiate paper is now in its twenty-eighth year. It has never changed its name, but in memory of the past is still known as *Madisonensis*. It is issued bi-weekly, is edited with enterprise, and holds honorable rank among college papers.

For some time after the reconstruction in 1850, the university drew its teaching force mainly from among its own alumni. This state of things gradually passed away, however. At present, the faculties of instruction include twenty-five men in actual service (not counting instructors), and among them are found graduates from twelve different colleges. The university has been nobly served by its own sons, and yet it has never had one of its alumni for its president, and at present has only one in its theological faculty. The ruling desire in the present period is to draw upon resources of both kinds: to utilize the power and loyalty of its own graduates, and yet to be drawing in fresh life from beyond itself. It is certain that recent years have witnessed a great quickening and enlargement of the general life of the place, and that such a reviving, once begun, will not die away.

MU OF DELTA KAPPA EPSILON.

The Delta Kappa Epsilon Fraternity was founded in 1844 at Yale, where scholarship had been almost the sole standard in societies, with the intention of combining in the standard of the new order the scholarly, the manly, and the social. The new fraternity made rapid progress, and Mu, established within twelve years, became its seventeenth chapter.

The early history of Mu is of romantic interest. When the chapter was founded secret societies were under the ban. The fears of the Faculty saw in them a menace to scholarship and morality. Expulsion being the penalty of discovery, there was necessary the utmost secrecy. Mystery and danger, however, quickened the loyalty of the little band, and lent added charm to their meetings. The boys still delight to gather around an honored veteran of those early days and listen with breathless interest as he recounts the story, Othello-like, "of most disastrous chances, of moving accidents, of hair-breadth 'scapes, of being taken by the insolent foe." As the existence of

the chapter gradually became known, opposition slowly subsided and Mu of Δ. Υ. acquired the proud distinction of winning the right of existence in the university for secret societies.

With the growth of membership and influence the oft-expressed desire for a hall crystalized into action. The excavation was made and the foundations laid at the cost of great labor by the active members, while alumni helped the work along by generous subscriptions. In January, 1877, the first regular meeting was held in the present ivy-clad temple. The memories which cluster round "the little house by the creek" are warmly cherished by every Δ. Υ. Its walls have rung with pealing laughter and stirring eloquence, and around its glowing fireside hearts have been knit together in closest brotherhood.

In 1892 an epoch in the history of the chapter was marked by the gift from Mr. Francis T. Pierce, '57, of a delightful chapter home as a memorial of his only son, Frank Burchard Pierce, '86, the inspiration of whose life and the pathos of whose early death have left a permanent impress upon the chapter he loved. The house is a charming home, and is filled by as merry a family as ever sang around a hearthstone.

As the oldest chapter in the university, Mu has always maintained a strong position. It has striven to be faithful to the original intention of the fraternity to which it belongs, and to maintain a good standard in scholarship, in character, and in society.

DELTA UPSILON.

The Delta Upsilon Chapter House was erected in 1882, and was one of the first buildings in the United States to combine the idea of a hall for meeting purposes with that of a chapter home. The site was purchased for $2,000, and the building of red brick, beautiful in its architectural design, was completed in 1893 by the erection of a commodious addition at a total cost of $15,000. It is to the praise of the society that out of many modest contributions the chapter house was raised as a monument to the unselfish love and loyalty of Delta Upsilon alumni. The house contains rooms, mostly in suites of two, for sixteen men; it has a commodious dining-room, a well equipped culinary department, and ample accommodations for its matron and servants, while its spacious parlor, hall, and library, all opening into one, make its reception rooms unsurpassed. On the second floor is the assembly hall with a seating capacity of 150, in which the conclaves of the chapter and entertainments for friends and alumni are held. The house is in reality the home of the chapter, and the rec-

ollections of happy hours spent around the glowing embers in cracking jokes and singing the old songs will be among the happiest memories of college life.

The Colgate chapter, organized in 1865, is one of the 33 chapters of the Delta Upsilon fraternity which was founded at Williams College in 1834. At first the society was anti-secret, but in time changed to non-secret.

Social entertainments form no small part of the chapter life at Colgate, and the house is recognized as a centre of social life. The chapter has always insisted upon high class standing in its members, and its honors in scholarship have been many. The society has been true to its early ideals, and has enjoyed a prosperous career. Its aim has ever been "To secure the union of college men of finished tastes for the promotion of social, intellectual and moral culture."

The fraternity is represented in the university and town by President G. W. Smith, Professors W. H. Maynard, J. M. Taylor, J. F. McGregory, A. P. Brigham, R. W. Thomas, A. C. McGiffert, W. F. Langworthy, E. H. Howard, W. T. White, J. P. Foster, Treasurer W. R. Rowlands, the Rev. C. S. Sargent, and Dr. G. S. Langworthy.

PHI KAPPA PSI FRATERNITY

A history of New York Epsilon of Phi Kappa Psi would be incomplete if it failed to take into account the local society with

battle for the existence of a fourth organization in our University and prepared the way for the present chapter.

Æonia was the name chosen by one of the two local societies formed in 1846. It continued as part of the University life until 1873, when it went out of existence. In the fall of 1880 the society was reorganized. The meeting places were Alumni Hall, East College, and later a hall in the Smith Block.

The disadvantages of a local society soon became painfully apparent, and when in 1886 two members from New York Beta of Phi Kappa Psi, situated at Syracuse University, came to Colgate, and suggested that the society should apply for a charter, vague ideas became definite at once, and a spirit of conservatism was developed.

On April 29, 1887, the local society, which had won high standing in the face of great disadvantages, went out of existence, and a new chapter of Phi Kappa Psi was formed by brothers from Syracuse and Cornell.

The chapter retained the rooms into which Æonia had moved. These rooms were situated in the Tripp Block on Lebanon Street.

The first five years of chapter life were uneventful. Delegates to District Councils and Grand Arch Councils kept the chapter in touch with the fraternity life as a whole.

In 1892 the present chapter house was built. There had been a growing desire and determination to build, and this culminated in the spring of 1892. The chapter house is the headquarters of the chapter life. Nearly all the members board here and many room in the building.

Phi Kappa Psi at Colgate has won and is maintaining her place of honor among the Fraternities here represented. The fraternity stands for the development of well-rounded manhood, and whatever tends to promote this object receives encouragement from the life of the chapter.

The position of the chapter on the question of the number of members is neither conservative nor radical. The number of charter members was eighteen. The present membership is twenty-eight.

THETA PSI OF PHI GAMMA DELTA

The fraternity of Phi Gamma Delta was founded in 1848 at Washington and Jefferson College, James G. Blaine, then a student there, being prominent in its organization.

There are now forty-six active and eleven graduate chapters. The governing power is vested in a Grand Chapter located in New York City. Among the prominent alumni may be mentioned Gen. Lew

Wallace, diplomat and novelist, John Clark Ridpath, historian, Edward Eggleston, novelist, Bishop McLaren of the Episcopal Church, and President Dabney of the University of Tennessee.

The Colgate chapter was established in 1887, with eight charter members. From the first its progress has been uniform and constant. Its aim has been to secure men who unite the qualities of character, scholarship and congeniality. Deprecating the tendency noticeable in some quarters to make a fraternity merely a social club, it has always emphasized literary training. A large number of scholastic and college honors have been won by its members, and they have been well represented in all other phases of college life.

From its formation in 1889 until 1891 the chapter occupied rooms in the Smith block. It then removed to the Mott block, where it remained until the spring of 1894, when the present house on Madison street was secured. It is well adapted to the needs of the society, containing, on the ground floor, double parlors, dining-room, kitchen, bath room, and matron's suite of rooms. Above these are accommodations for twelve men. The house is heated by furnace, and has hot and cold water throughout.

We think that anyone who has chanced to pass the house on a spring evening, and has heard the notes of some old college song swelling in unison with the sweet vibrations of mandolin and guitar, or the banjo's soulful plunk, will agree with us that there are no jollier fellows in Colgate than the Fijis.

HISTORY OF THE COLGATE CHAPTER OF BETA THETA PI

The history of the Colgate chapter, the Beta Theta of Beta Theta Pi, strictly speaking, covers a period of fifteen years. The chapter was founded December 10, 1880. It is the representative of the old Adelphian Society which, after an honorable and useful existence of forty years, became, on the date named, a chapter of the Beta Theta Pi fraternity. The Adelphian Society carried into the new relations all its active members and all its possessions, including a library of nearly one thousand volumes especially rich in poetry, history and periodical literature.

The chapter has changed its quarters several times. It was at first located in the Smith block, but soon secured rooms in the Dodge block, and in January, 1893, removed to the president's old mansion on the hill. This has continued to be the home of the chapter.

A strong conservative spirit in regard to membership has been manifested from the beginning. There were thirty-nine charter mem-

bers. The smallest active membership during any one college year was eleven, in 1884-85; at one time during the year there were only seven members. The largest membership was twenty-nine, in the college year of 1880-81. The present active chapter is composed of twenty-four men.

The achievements of the alumni, in the various walks of life, signify that they are men of energy and ability. The whole number of alumni is one hundred and nine. The majority are in the ministry. The next largest number is engaged in educational work, occupying positions from the academic professor to the college president. Others are engaged in journalism, Y. M. C. A. work, and in the practice of law and medicine.

The active chapter has ever held a prominent place in scholarship and in the literary work of the college. We are also well represented in the social, musical and athletic life of the students. While the chapter encourages friendly rivalry, which develops the innate possibilities of its members, it does not sacrifice for success the ideals of true manhood. The fraternity believes in manliness, fairness, charity, and universal brotherhood. These principles are knit into an inward history in the life of each Beta, binding us together with bonds that cannot be severed while memory lasts.

"EMILY JUDSON" HALL

Boarding and Day School for Young Ladies

"Emily Judson" Hall opened Sept. 12, 1895, for College Preparatory Courses, with Electives in Literature, History, English, Domestic Science, Physical Culture, Art, and Music. Special training is given in Greek and Latin Composition; ear-training in French and German; original work in Geometry; and special work in English Composition. Graduates of Academies may elect studies, either to strengthen their preparation for college, or for a "finishing year." Mature women also, may here find an opportunity for study. Since life in a boarding school may give tone to one's whole after life, care is taken to give true womanly ideals. Through the "Fanny Forrester" club, the pupils are also taught to work in organizations. The school though unsectarian, is distinctly Christian, and memorializes in its name Emily Judson, a teacher, writer, and missionary, and a resident of Hamilton. The Dormitory is heated by steam and equipped with modern improvements. The site is desirable. Summer courses in Music and Art. Piano, including harmony and counter-point Leipsic. Voice, including sight reading, voice-building.

ballad and Church music (New Eng. Conservatory) ; Art, including field-work (Vassar). The Dormitory will be opened for boarders at reasonable rates. For further particulars address Mrs. Mary Davis Moore, Principal.

Mrs. Moore refers by permission to—Dr. G. W. Smith, Pres. Colgate University ; Prof. E. P. Sisson, Prin. Colgate Academy ; Dr. E. A. Sheldon, Prin. Oswego Normal School ; Hon. C. R. Skinner, State Supt. of Instruction ; Hon. D. Ainsworth, Deputy Supt. of Instruction ; Prof. C. H. Thurber, Prin. Morgan Park Academy, Chicago ; Prin. Leonard, Binghamton High School ; Mrs. Myron Goodenough, Hamilton ; Hon. W. H. Corbin, Elizabeth, N. J. ;

"Emily Jutson" Hall.

Clark H. Gleason, Esq., Grand Rapids, Mich. ; Mr. D. C. Heath, Boston, and others.

THE NATIONAL HAMILTON BANK

The "Hamilton Bank," organized under the laws of the State of New York, commenced business in January, 1853. First Board of Directors: Adon Smith, Henry Tower, John Mott, Lewis Wickwire, Alvah Pierce, John J. Foote, Delos DeWolf, Artemas Osgood, D. B. West, Smith Mott, William Felt, Alonzo Peck, and William Cobb. First President, Adon Smith ; First Vice President, Alvah Pierce ; First Cashier, D. B. West, who continued to be an active officer of the bank and its successor until his death, which occurred January 3d, 1864. Reorganized under the National Bank act May, 1865. New title: "The National Hamilton Bank." Charter expired in May, 1885, and was renewed for twenty years. Board of Directors now, 1896: B. F. Bonney, F. T. Pierce, D. G. Wellington, Sidney D. Smith, George H. Barker, Hervey E. Eaton, William M. West, Adon N. Smith, and Leroy Fairchild. Officers: William M. West, President; Adon N. Smith, Vice-President; Leroy Fairchild, Cashier; Charles J. Griswold, Assistant Cashier; Bookkeeper, John J. Taylor.

THE NEW BANK BUILDING.

The new National Hamilton Bank building, in architectural design, construction, finish, furnishings, and adaptability to the purposes for which it was designed, has no superior or, for that matter equal, in Central New York. The details and arrangement of the bank offices proper, together with the selection of their furnishings, were the work of Gen. William M. West, and are a splendid monument of his taste and of the knowledge gleaned from his years of experience in banking affairs. With the arrangement of the bank offices determined upon by Gen. West, Mr. O. K. Foote, of Rochester, was selected to draft the building plans for the new edifice, and that able architect has given us an enduring specimen of the art which has made the city from which he hails the envy of her sister cities and the pride of Western New York.

The building stands at the corner of Madison and Broad streets, and occupies the site of the burned Gaskell building. It is of irregular width but the average dimensions are about 75 by 40 feet. The material used in its construction, from grade to and including second story sill course, is rock finish St. Lawrence marble. The second and third stories — the building is a three story one — have fronts of mottled gray pressed brick, which were furnished by the New York Hydraulic-Press Brick Company. The window sills are St. Lawrence marble, and the main entrance same material with cut finish. The

cornice is copper and elegant in design. All windows are of heavy plate glass and a metal roof covers all. The sidewalk is manufactured... Fireproof is... construction the ceiling in arches of... steel... concrete. The... floor is built on... construction... sidewalk. A highly ornamental... and... is... use... of design. The first floor and basement are occupied entirely by... the second... third floors by... Every part of the interior of this splendid building furnishes a practical illustration of the possibilities obtainable from a judicious combination of... taste, science and skill. A. B. Carman, of Bing-

are the best burglar proof safes, only on a larger scale. In its construction nearly fifty tons of steel and iron were used. The outside door alone weighs nearly thirteen thousand pounds; the inner door about eight thousand pounds. The outer door is furnished with the Burton-Harris automatic locking device controlled by a three-movement time lock, and is without any sort of hole or opening through it. The inner door has two of the best known combination locks, controlled by a two-movement chronometer lock. The safe deposit boxes are of the very latest construction and are protected by both doors mentioned above. The vault is a perfect revelation of mechanism and cannot but excite the admiration of the casual observer or the most skillful mechanic or designer. Doors weighing from four to six and a half tons each are made by ball-bearing adjustments to swing as easily as the ordinary church doors; so perfectly are they fitted that when closed the vault is absolutely air tight and nothing can be inserted between the door and casing, while the entire absence of any openings through the outer door for the adjustment of knobs, combinations or other purposes, leaves the would-be burglar without a starting point upon which to operate. The locking devices, together with their chronometer controlment are so perfect and all accidents thereto so amply provided for that a failure to work with exact precision seems an utter impossibility. But if an entrance could be effected through the seemingly impassable doors or walls of the vault, the burglar would still be confronted with plenty of work before his purpose would be accomplished. To open the safety deposit boxes by unlocking, he must have two keys, one of which is in the hands of the depositor, the other in the keeping of the bank, and neither key will unlock a box without the use of the other. Without the aid of the keys all the ingenuity of the skilled burglar would be required to gain access to the boxes. If the bank's money was wanted it would have to be obtained by opening one of the very best burglar-proof safes, which has been placed inside of the vault.

In the basement, directly underneath the vault described, is another large fire-proof vault for the storage of property belonging to the bank or its customers. This vault is larger, stronger, better, than the famous vault in the burned bank building on Lebanon street, which furnished indisputable proof that fire could not harm it, and which afterwards, for sometime, almost defied the efforts of the workmen employed to remove it. Impervious to man's efforts or the elements, as these vaults seemingly are, they too are guarded, not alone by a building of fire-proof construction, but by every detail that enters into the design of the building. Not a door or window has been placed in the structure without first considering its position with regard to the safety of the vaults. So successful have the designers been in the accomplishment of their desires that no entrance to the bank can be obtained that will not bring the intruder at any hour of the night, into the full glare of electric lights on the first floor and into the presence of those left on guard.

WILLIAM RANDALL ROWLANDS.

Mr. Rowlands was born in 1853, near Hamilton. He was graduated from Colgate University in 1874. In 1878 he took a trip to Europe, and he has visited many parts of our own country. During

the year 1880-81 he took a graduate course at Yale University. Mrs. Rowlands accompanied him and pursued a course of study at the Yale Art School.

For one year Mr. Rowlands was Professor of Mathematics and Assistant Principal of the Medina Academy. The following four years he was principal of the Hamilton Union School. His last graduating class, 1880, of 31 members, was the largest in the history of the school.

For one year, 1874-75, he had the advantage of early experience in business in New York city. In 1881 he engaged in business in Utica. He erected the Rowlands Building, one of the finest office structures in Central New York. He was chairman of the Citizens' Committee that secured the nomination of Charles H. Searle for mayor, and he was instrumental in organizing the Immanuel and the Calvary Baptist Churches of Utica, and has done much to aid them. For

Residence of William R. Rowlands.

several years previous to returning to Hamilton, he was president of the Young Men's Christian Association of Utica, and was chairman of the committee when the new Association building, one of the finest in this country, was constructed. He served in many other positions of responsibility and honor.

In 1889 he accepted the treasurership of Colgate University. In the same week in which he entered upon his new duties, the Immanuel Church building of Utica, which he had done so much to secure, was dedicated; also the exercises at the opening of the Utica Young Men's building, just completed, were held. Few young men, with so short a residence, have left the city of Utica under pleasanter circumstances and with greater honors.

Mr. Rowlands was chairman of the committee that erected the Delta Upsilon House at Colgate, and was the resident member of the building committee for the new Colgate gymnasium. He recently built his residence and is planning to erect a block in the "burned district" the coming spring.

For nearly nine years Mr. Rowlands has been a member of the State Committee of the Young Men's Christian Association and a member of the sub-committee on colleges. In 1886-87 he was acting president of the National Fraternity of Delta Upsilon. Recently he was elected corresponding member of the Oneida Historical Society.

SMITH BUILDING

The enterprise shown by the well known firm of Smith Brothers,

Residence of Adon N. Smith.

(consisting of Sidney D. Smith, Arthur J. Smith, Adon N. Smith and Mrs. D. M. Fairchild,) after the great fire of February 19th, 1895, can be seen by the cut on the preceding page. The ruins of the old Smith block were hardly cold before they planned the handsome new building which now stands on the site of the former block. Work was begun on March 11th to clean up the ruins of the fire, the first bricks were laid on May 16th, and the building completed (except the inside finishing) on July 30th. Mr. Adon N. Smith was the first to occupy a store in the new building, which he did on August 31st. The rest of the tenants were all in by October 1st. The building is a massive brick structure of three stories and contains ten stores, nine flats, Masonic Hall, Banquet Hall, Grotto Hall, Ball Room, Club rooms, and six finely appointed offices. The building has all modern improvements, and is a great credit to the business enterprise of the firm as well as a pride to the citizens of Hamilton.

C. B. SANFORD
Jeweler and Optician

In March, 1895, Mr. C. B. Sanford succeeded to the jewelry business which was established by A. G. Sanford in 1868. The store is located in the Davis block, Lebanon street, where Mr. Sanford has ample accommodations for conducting his business. His stock of watches, jewelry, silverware and novelties is choice and complete.

Mr. Sanford being an expert optician, carries a full line of optical supplies. In the line of fine watch repairing, Mr. Sanford is considered one of the best workmen in Hamilton. He is a gentleman whom it is a pleasure to meet.

ADON N. SMITH
Hardware, Plumbing, Steam Fitting and Roofing

Among Hamilton's business enterprises, none is more prominent than the extensive hardware establishment conducted by Adon N. Smith, founded in 1885, and now located in the south store of the "Smith Building." The stock carried is very large and comprehensive, and includes a complete line of heavy and shelf goods, agricultural implements, stoves, ranges, furnaces, etc. Mr. Smith is the selling agent for several of the most celebrated makes. One of the special features of this house is plumbing, roofing and general jobbing in tin, copper and sheet iron work ; the best of workmen are employed and satisfaction is always guaranteed.

The interior fittings and furnishings of Mr. Smith's establishment are of the finest, and every feature of the store is arranged for convenience in conducting his business. Mr. Smith is one of Hamilton's most enterprising and prominent merchants. He is associated with its

banking and several other business interests, while socially and fraternally he is connected with Hamilton's best.

HAMLIN & CO.
Druggists and Pharmacists, Opera House Block

This is one of the leading and most reliable establishments of the kind in Hamilton. It is a complete and first class drug store, where physicians' prescriptions and family recipes are compounded in the most careful and accurate manner from fresh ingredients. This popular firm was established in 1895, and from its inception the venture has proved a highly gratifying success. The store is finely fitted up and tastefully arranged. The copartners exercise close personal supervision over their business. A large first class stock is constantly

carried, including everyth...   ...es and medic...
the standard propr...tary m...
sides a full line of p...
ties. The firm...   M.. ... H...   ...Dr. O...
Langworthy, the...

GEORGE BEAL.
Hamilton's Popular Postmaster

Among the representative pe... Ha...ton...
Mr. George Beal, Hamilton'...   ...Sep...
1894, this gentleman was app...

during the administra...   ...he has proved h...
ably competent...   ...t...
ing cir..mstan...   Mr. B...
become familiar with th...
complications wh...
with the except...ed of a...

very little was lost. To illustrate Mr. Beal's remarkable executive ability, business was resumed at once in Paterson's shoe shop on Lebanon street, every mail was dispatched on time, and but one mail was delayed in distribution. After the fire a temporary office was established in Mr. Mott's residence on Broad street, until a building was erected in Shanty Town, where business was transacted until Mr. Beal took possession of the elegantly equipped office now occupied in the Smith building. While the office here is rated in the third class, the business transacted in money orders alone is much larger than in many second class offices. Mr. Beal, who is a gentleman in the prime of life, was born and reared in Hamilton. Aside

Interior of Post-office.

from his position as postmaster, he is also a member of the firm of Rowlands & Beal, furniture dealers and undertakers. Mr. Beal is also prominently identified with fraternal and social organizations. He is District Deputy G. M. of the 17th Masonic district, and is altogether one of Hamilton's leading citizens.

F. N. TOMPKINS

Watches and Jewelry.

The trade in watches, diamonds and jewelry has a very satisfactory representative in this village in Mr. F. N. Tompkins, who established himself in business here in 1880. Mr. Tompkins is intimately familiar with all the details of the trade in which he is engaged, and sustains relations of the most favorable character with manufacturers and leading wholesale houses for the purchase of his supplies. His store is replete with a superior assortment of gold and silver watches of the leading makes, diamonds in elegant settings, and a complete variety of jewelry of every description, all well worthy of inspection. As a business man Mr. Tompkins is energetic and progressive, and has met with a success which his merits fully deserve.

DAVID H. FOSTER
Insurance

With the breaking out of the war of the Rebellion in 1861, Mr. Foster was among the first to respond to the call for volunteers. At the age of 18 he enlisted in the 75th Regiment at Auburn, N. Y., and served with distinction three years, during all of which time he was in active service, receiving three promotions and commissions. In 1864 he was engaged as manager of the office of Collector of Internal Revenue, which office he occupied in three different districts, covering a term of 14 years. The office in this, the 22d district of N. Y., became under his management the foremost in the State of New York, and was mentioned in the report of the Examiner and Supervisor of Internal Revenue, as the best managed in the State. When the districts were finally consolidated throughout the State, and the office of the 22d district turned over, the accounts, which had covered millions of dollars, were found to balance to a cent.

In 1870, Mr. Foster engaged in the business of Fire Insurance, and became prominent as most active, prompt, and reliable in this, as in all his other business transactions. As general insurance agent and adjuster of fire losses, there is probably no agent who enjoys a wider acquaintance and patronage.

By his thorough knowledge of insurance, coupled with a high regard for integrity and fairness, Mr. Foster has built up one of the largest and most popular agencies in Central New York. He repre-

Residence of D. H. Foster.

sents the oldest, strongest and best insurance companies in the world, embracing fire, life, and accident.

This agency paid more losses in each of the three conflagrations that visited Canastota, Earlville, and Hamilton in this county, than any other, and stands higher and stronger than ever. Mr. Foster has a fine office in the new "Smith Building"; and like his fine residence shown in the above cut, it is fitted with all the modern conveniences of steam heat, plumbing, and electric lights. Mr. Foster is enterprising, liberal, and one of the foremost citizens of Hamilton.

NICHOLS & BEAL
Druggists and Grocers

The house of Messrs. Nichols & Beal, known as the Pioneer drug store, is rightly named, as it is one of the oldest mercantile establishments in Hamilton, having been founded by Joseph Mott in 1822. The present firm was organized in 1892. The copartners are thoroughly familiar with the business in which they are engaged, and from the inception of their enterprise secured a strong hold on public favor, and have been the recipients of a very influential patronage. Their store is very handsomely arranged with every convenience for the transaction of business. Realizing the importance of their large

The Nichols & Beal Block

and increasing prescription trade, they have prepared a separate department for their compounding, in which will be found all the latest improved devices for securing accuracy and precision. The stock embraces pure and fresh drugs, chemicals and pharmaceutical preparations, all of which are up to the highest standard assured by the United States Pharmacopœia. In a different branch of retirement, they also deal in paints, oils, varnishes, glass and painters' supplies, and carry at all times a full line of groceries, fine imported and domestic cigars, fruits, and confectionery. In the store is also the office of the Western Union Telegraph Company.

The Nichols & Beal block in which the store is located, is one of the architectural features of Hamilton. The building is a three-

Nichols & Beal's Drug Store.

story brick structure, is heated by hot water and lighted by electricity. The inside finishings are of the best class, and the building throughout is a model of completeness. Mr. O. S. Nichols, who is secretary and treasurer of the Hamilton Social Club, is also identified with other organizations. Mr. Thos. H. Beal, is one of the governors of the Hamilton Social Club. He is prominently connected with the fire department and also in Masonic circles.

Interior of L. M. Royce's Store.

L. M. ROYCE
Dealer in Crockery, Groceries, &c.

Established in 1871 by its present proprietor, with location on the site now occupied, this house has steadily maintained its prestige in the trade, and increased the scope of its trade operations from year to year, until to-day the house is recognized as one of the most prominent in its line in this section.

The store, which is a credit to Hamilton, is commodious and neatly arranged, while an extensive line of goods is carried in every department. On entering the store the visitor finds on every hand beauti-

Residence L. M. Royce

ful china and porcelain wares, lamps, rare crockery, china dinner and tea sets, wall papers and ceiling decorations, &c.

The grocery department is also completely equipped, and embraces every article coming under the head of staple and fancy groceries, while everything is of the best quality. The proprietor, Mr. L. M. Royce, who is a liberal and enterprising business man, was reared in Sauquoit, Oneida county, and resided there until August, 1862, when he enlisted in the army and served his country faithfully until 1865. After receiving his discharge he took up his residence in Chadwicks, Oneida county, remaining there until 1868, when he moved to Lee, Mass., and there engaged in the mercantile business. In 1871 he came to Hamilton and conducted a hardware store for five years, after which he embarked in his present business. Throughout his career as a merchant he has been remarkably successful. He enjoys a large trade throughout the village and vicinity by reason of the generous treatment accorded patrons. He is a representative of the Village Improvement Association, and is closely allied with the industrial advancement of Hamilton.

SHELDON OPERA HOUSE
E. B. Sheldon, Proprietor and Manager

Hamilton is adequately provided with a place of amusement in the Sheldon Opera House. This edifice was erected during the past year,

Sheldon Opera House.

and was opened to the public on September 24th, 1895, by the Artists' Quartette of Boston. The Sheldon Opera House occupies a massive brick building containing three stories, one of which is occupied by Mr. Sheldon for conducting his extensive grocery business. The theatre is on the ground floor, and occupies the main part of the building, while dispersed through the building are several handsome offices. The Opera House is furnished with all modern improvements, and is lighted by electricity. The house is divided into dress circle and balcony. There are five dressing rooms, heated, under the stage. The theater has a seating capacity of about 1,000. The

equipments include patent folding chairs, while the interior decorations of the house are such as to make it a model in every respect. The stage is 30x60 feet in dimension, its height from floor to fly iron is 8 feet, the curtain opening 24x26 feet. The house is supplied with six different sets of scenery. Mr. Sheldon, who is a native of the village of Madison, Lake county, moved to Hamilton in his youth, and for the past twenty years has been for a number of firms chant, he and family being well known for their social qualities throughout the northern part of the county. He is a member of the H plan. The opera house together with...
The house is admirably fitted up and arranged in every respect

state. Both among the profession and the public Mr. Sheldon has gained a high reputation for his own line of business.

ROWLANDS & BEAL.
Furniture and Undertaking

Among the prominent mercantile enterprises of Hamilton is direct to the of Mr. Rowlands & Beal, established about 1875, Park & Garfield. In 1876, Rowlands & Beal succeeded to the business. The firm is now equipped in the Davis Block on Lebanon street, which they occupy entirely. In Sept. 1892 Moses Rowlands & Beal will open up...

Rowlands building.

show rooms in the building represented by the accompanying cut, and to be erected by William R. Rowlands. The firm at present carries a stock embracing everything that may be desired in fine and

Rowlands & Beal's Store.

medium furniture, chamber suits, parlor sets, dining-room, library and hall furniture, &c. All goods are purchased from leading jobbers and are offered to the public at lowest prices. It has always been the aim of this house to furnish such furniture as should rank superior in quality of material, finish, and workmanship. In all respects this well known house occupies a leading position in the trade of Hamilton. This firm is the leading undertaking establishment in this section, and gives special attention to this branch of the business, Mr. W. W. Ray having charge as funeral director and embalmer. Mr. Ray's many years experience in his line assures perfect arrangement of all matters entrusted to him.

Park House.

The members of the firm are J. W. Rowlands and George Beal, both are highly respected citizens. They are closely identified with the growth and development of Hamilton, and have done much to foster and enhance its welfare and prosperity.

W. G. LIPPITT
Proprietor Park House

Hamilton contains some really excellent hotels. Among these the popular Park House, presided over by Mr. W. G. Lippitt, occupies a high place in the esteem of the traveling and local public. The

Park House Office.

Park House is one of the landmarks of Hamilton; it was built in 1807, and has been conducted as a hotel ever since. The house has been remodeled and improved at various times, and under Mr. Lippitt's proprietorship many improvements have been made, notably

Park House Bar

those in the office, which is as complete as that of any first-class city hotel. The house throughout is one of the most attractive and cozy hotels hereabouts. The table set at the Park House is unsurpassed.

Mr. Lippitt is a native of Hamilton, but resided in Norwich from 1881 until he took possession of this house, May 6th, 1894. Prior to engaging in the hotel business he conducted a jewelry store at Norwich.

The old Park House has certainly fallen into the hands of one who will add lustre to its fame as a well-conducted and homelike hotel.

HOTEL MAXWELL.
M. F. Maxwell, Proprietor

Hamilton is favored with the advantages and benefits derived from the location here of one of the finest modern hotels in Central New

York. We refer to the Hotel Maxwell, which has such an enviable reputation with all who have partaken of its bountiful hospitality. This hotel was erected by Mr. Maxwell in the spring of 1895. It stands three stories high, and is a substantial modern brick structure. Making a tour of the hotel we find on the first floor a handsome office and reading room, a restaurant, and elegantly equipped dining-room. The ceilings are Neer Gager's steel ceilings, which are acknowledged the finest steel ceilings made, while the wood work is of quartered oak, and is finely finished. The upper floors contain elegantly furnished parlors and sitting-rooms, besides twenty finely appointed sleeping rooms, single and en suite. The house is heated by a hot water system, lighted by electricity and supplied with electric bells. In the rear of the house is an iron fire escape reaching from the dome to the ground. This is of itself a feature which is highly regarded by the traveling public. Mr. Maxwell is an expert in every detail, and is fully conversant with all modern requirements regarding hotel-keeping. The Hotel Maxwell surpasses in beauty and equipment all other hotels in this section, and is a popular resort for both commercial men and families. Mr. Maxwell is a liberal caterer, believes in the best and plenty of it, while the cuisine is in charge of competent assistants. Mr. Maxwell is a typical Boniface, pleasant

Hotel Maxwell Office.

mannered, active and energetic, and is well calculated to conduct successfully an establishment of this kind, as is amply attested by his judicious management of the Hotel Maxwell.

MRS. J. G. ABEL & CO.
Cash Department Store, Smith Building

The above business was inaugurated in 1880 by the late J. G. Abel, and conducted by him until his death in 1890. Following that the business was operated under his estate, and in 1895 the firm of Mrs. J. G. Abel & Co. succeeded to the business. The copartners are Mrs. J. G. Abel and Mrs. F. A. Staples, while Mr. R. W. Hulburd is also associated with the firm. The class of goods handled embraces every variety of crockery, glassware, silver plated ware, cutlery, complete line of stationery and school supplies, tin and hollow ware toys, household specialties, house furnishings and fancy in fact everything is kept to be found in a first class bazaar. A special feature is made of carrying in stock a full line of staple and fancy groceries, fruits and confectionery, the house being headquarters for select teas and coffees. This department is in charge of Mr. Hulburd, who has a wide experience in the tea, coffee, and grocery trade. The premises occupied in the Smith building are of ample dimensions, and are well equipped for carrying on the business. We also make mention that the telephone and Adams express

offices are located in this store. The copartners of the cash department store are fully conversant with every detail of the business in which they are engaged, and we recommend them to the patronage of our readers.

N. R. WICKWIRE

Wholesale and Retail Dealer in Flour, Feed, Grain, Masons' Supplies, &c.

An extensive trade is carried on here in Flour and Grain, and among the firms considered prominent and influential in the business is the well known house of Mr. N. R. Wickwire. The business was established in 1882, and a trade has been built up which has proved lucrative and satisfactory. The business is steadily growing and expanding under the able management of Mr. Wickwire, whose experience in this special line has been comprehensive. The transactions are marked by a fair and liberal policy, and the connections are of the most satisfactory character. All demands are promptly met.

Mr. Wickwire is a trustee of the Public School Board, also a member of the Citizen's Club, besides being identified with fraternal organizations. He is a progressive business man and a credit to this community.

Residence of N. R. Wickwire.

VALENTINE PIOTROW
Merchant Tailor and Men's Furnishings

In 1860 Mr. Piotrow organized his present business, which has gained a wide reputation for fine work and reliable business methods. The new block erected by him since the fire is nicely arranged for the conducting of his growing business. F. W. Piotrow, his son, is a cutter of many years' experience. He is also connected with several of Hamilton's fraternal and social organizations. Both are gentlemen of good business ability, and stand well in business and social life.

Residence — Dr. Lloyd.

F. O. Lloyd, A. M., M. D., a regular physician, is an adopted son of Hamilton, having come to the village in 1877. He was graduated from Colgate University with the class of 1881, and entering upon the study of medicine received the degree of M. D. from the University of the City of New York in 1885. He was the Valedictorian of his class. Special study, in various lines, under Dr. A. L. Loomis, Dr. W. H. Thomson and Dr. Herman Knapp; one year of residence in the Newark City Hospital as House Physician and Surgeon, and several months of travel abroad followed graduation; and then Dr. Lloyd settled in New York City for the practice of his profession. During the five years of his practice in New York, he received appointments as Attending Physician to the Northwestern Dispensary, Attending Physician to the Demilt Dispensary, Attending Physician to the Presbyterian Hospital, Attending Physician and Surgeon to the Baptist Home, and Lecturer at the Postgraduate Medical College. Ill-health compelled a residence of a year in Colorado in 1892-93. On returning east eminent specialists advised Dr. Lloyd not to subject himself to the unhealthful conditions of the city and he, therefore, settled in Hamilton in 1893, where he continues the practice of medicine.

A. L. L. HALL

Music Dealer

The scene below represents the interior of Hall's Music Rooms. Mr. Hall, its proprietor, is a young man who, in the few months of Hamilton's new existence, has built up a large and increasing trade. The secret of his success lies in his policy, "Good goods at fair profit." The fact that the Knabe, Briggs, and other pianos are sold here, at prices rivalling those of the largest houses in the State, is but another indication of the characteristic Hamilton push. Mr. Hall's music rooms are located in the Opera House Block.

A. L. L. Hall's Store.

W. W. FELT

Livery and Boarding Stable

In the rear of the Park House are the Livery, Sales, and Boarding Stables of Mr. W. W. Felt, who has been engaged in the business for the past 14 years, and has during all that time occupied his present location. The premises are extensive and contain a two story building, thoroughly lighted and ventilated, and perfect as regards sanitary arrangements. A number of first-class horses, buggies, carriages, hacks, barouches, sleighs, light wagons, &c., are kept constantly on hand for hire at reasonable prices, and elegant turnouts with careful drivers are supplied promptly for funerals, wedding parties, &c., at all hours of the day or night. Mr. Folt h... some of the finest coach teams to be seen anywhere. A p... feature is made of boarding h... on the most favorable terms and the stock is g... in the best of ca... expe... ... and stable men. Mr. Folt does ... ... trade. He ... born in Earlville but has resided in Hamilt... ... he was ... y years of ...

FRANK TUMAN

Shaving Parlor and Billiards

Of the numerous enterprises of Hamilton deserving of favorable recognition in this review is the establishment conducted by Mr. F. Tuman, who occupies finely equipped quarters in his modern building on Lebanon street. The building is a three-story brick structure and it can be safely said that for exterior or interior equipments, no... tablishment of the kind in this part of the state compares with it for the purpose to which it is devoted. Making ... tour of the establishment the visitor finds on the first floor a very finely app... ate... ...ber shop, supplied with three chairs ... the latest improved pattern, while the fixtures throughout are of the best. In the rear of the barber shop are bath rooms, also a finely equipped billiard r... ... in the basement are two bowling alleys while the upper floors are used for residential purposes. Th... building ... heated by ... and

Tinman's Barber Shop.

The Pair word Timian Block.

its entire equipment throughout is fully in keeping with Hamilton's best structures, and reflects the highest credit on Mr. Thurman's good taste and judgment. Mr. Thurman fully posted on every requirement regarding his business, is thoroughly and favorably known, and fully deserves the large and steadily popular patronage.

WM. A. ST. JOHN
Fire, Life and Accident Insurance

Located in a convenient office on the second floor of the Smith Opera House is the insurance office of Mr. Wm. A. St. John, a man who was born at Highland, Mich., in 1864. In the year ... Mr. St. John came to Hamilton and entered Colgate University, in which he was graduated with honor in 1887. He was then for some

Wm. A.

seven years connected with the insurance interests of H......... and in 1894, he opened an office on his own account. Mr. St. John represents some of the leading insurance companies of the world. His business methods are such as to command the fullest confidence of the community.

Socially, or in business, Mr. St. John is always a very pleasant and affable gentleman to meet.

B. J. STETSON
Lawyer

Mr. Stetson is a Madison county man by birth, born in ...... ville, N. Y., April 24th, 1857. He obtained his education in the ...... schools and by private study, and was admitted to the bar of the state at Binghamton, in May, 1865, and at Detroit, Mich., the same year. After a short period of practice in Michigan he returned to this state, and married Rosealia B. Green, daughter of Hall Green, Esq., of Brookfield, N. Y. Mr. Stimson has one son, Wm. D., the jeweler, who is now connected with F. N. Tompkins, of Hamilton.

In 1874 Mr. B. J. Stimson removed to Hamilton, and has since resided here. He is prominently connected with several fraternal organizations, is also a member of the board of education of this village.

Residence of Pr. J. Crawshaw.

J. F. ROGERS

Baker and Grocer

Located in the Russell block on Madison street, Mr. Rogers conducts a business which in its various lines is quite extensive. Mr. Rogers' long experience as a baker gives him an advantage not possessed by many. He carries a complete stock of bakestuffs, fine confectionery, fruits, etc., while in his grocery department can always be found a well assorted stock of staple and fancy groceries. For parties and receptions a specialty is made of furnishing ice cream and ices. Mr. Rogers is connected with several of Hamilton's fraternal organizations, and has the welfare of Hamilton at heart.

M. M. MOONEY
Meat Market

The market of Mr. Mooney, located at the corner of Lebanon street and Maple avenue, is always stocked with a choice line of prime beef, lamb, pork, veal, sausage and poultry in season. Mr. Mooney's knowledge of the provision business assures all who patronize him that they will get meats that are first class. By prompt and courteous treatment he has built up a very substantial business, and he well deserves it, as he is a very pleasant and affable gentleman.

CHARLES C. GULBRAN
Hardware, Roofing, &c.

The oldest established hardware store in the Chenango Valley is that conducted by Mr. Charles C. Gulbran. The business was founded by Mr. E. Foote many years ago. A successor to Mr. Foote was Mr. E. B. Gaskell, who assumed proprietorship in 1886. Mr. Gulbran was in the employ of Mr. Gaskell for many years. In March, 1895, he purchased the business from Mr. Gaskell, and for ten years prior to that time he was in the employ of Mr. Adon N. Smith. Mr. Gulbran occupies a commodious store in the Phoenix Block, Lebanon Street, which is filled with a large and complete stock of hardware, agricultural implements, dairy supplies, shelf hardware, cutlery, and in short everything to be found in a well conducted hardware store. A specialty is made of roofing and tinsmithing. The stoves, ranges and furnaces dealt in by Mr. Gulbran are the Novelty Parlor stoves and ranges, the Andes and Imperial, also the Richardson and Boynton hot air furnaces. These are the highest types of development in this manufacturing art. As regards efficiency of service, durability, economy of fuel, and artistic style and finish, they are as near perfection as it is possible for human ingenuity to attain. Mr. Gulbran is a business man of enterprise. Thorough acquaintance with every detail of the business in which he is engaged, and the ample resources possessed for filling all orders, have made the house a favorite one with the trade.

CARL BAUM & SONS
Clothing and Men's Furnishing Goods

Among the business firms of Hamilton who have established their various enterprises recently, we note that of Messrs. Carl Baum & Sons, merchant tailors, and dealers in ready-made clothing and men's furnishings. The senior member of the firm was employed by Mr. Piotrow for eighteen years. His son, C. W., has been identified with the business for five years, and his son L. P., was engaged in the capacity of salesman for three years with a leading furnishing goods house in New York City. Having a thorough knowledge of the business in all its phases, these gentlemen formed a copartnership in September, 1895, under the present firm name. They carry in stock ready-made clothing, and also a fine line of gentlemen's furnishing goods, making a leading specialty of custom tailoring. This department is under the supervision of Mr. C. W. Baum. The copartners attend to every detail of their business with a solicitude that insures entire satisfaction to their many friends.

Front of Stock's Store.

A. H. STOCK
Colgate Book Store

One of Hamilton's popular book stores is that conducted by Mr. A. H. Stock, located in the Sheldon Opera House block, Lebanon street. The stock of books, periodicals, stationery, office and school supplies is always full and complete. Mr. Stock gets all the latest publications as soon as they appear, and by close attention to business he has built up a very satisfactory trade. Mr. Stock was graduated from Madison (now Colgate) University in 1876, and preached for fifteen years. He came to Hamilton from New Jersey, and located here in business in 1894. He is considered one of Hamilton's enterprising and progressive merchants.

H. H. MATTERSON

Mr. Matterson is a dealer in carriages, wagons, sleighs, horse furnishing goods, and farming machinery. He has been engaged in this enterprise since 1887, and since the fire has established temporary quarters for his business in a building located at his residence on Maple ave. The display made is one of the best in this section. Harness of every description is also dealt in. Mr. Matterson has resided in Hamilton since 1888. He is a thoroughly active and progressive gentleman.

L. H. BURNSIDE

Adams Express Agent

Mr. Burnside was born in South New Berlin, Chenango county, N. Y., Dec. 17th, 1863. About Nov. 1st, 1890, he came to Hamilton as the agent of the N. Y. O. & W. Ry., which position he held for nearly three years, filling the place with satisfaction to the railroad company and credit to himself. About June 1st, 1893, the Adams Express Company extended its business over the N. Y. O. & W. Ry. lines, and engaged Mr. Burnside as its agent in Hamilton. The express business has largely increased under his efficient management, which speaks well for Mr. Burnside's enterprise.

H. H. HILL

Photographer

Among those engaged in the photographic art in this section and occupying a prominent position, is Mr. Hill of this place, whose reputation is widespread in consequence of the excellence and artistic character of his productions. Mr. Hill is an artist of ripe experience, rare skill and judgment, and is a thorough master of all the different methods and new processes that have recently been introduced in the art.

The gallery is provided with the latest and best appliances. The operating room is supplied with the largest and finest camera to be found in this section.

Mr. Hill is a native of Hamilton, was born in 1844, and opened his first gallery in 1864. For some ten years prior to the fire of last February he was located in the Davis block. When the Sheldon

Opera House block was completed he secured commodious quarters on the upper floor of that building.

Mr. Hill turns out first class work, and deserves the liberal patronage he receives.

E. WATTS CUSHMAN

Attorney and Counsellor

The subject of this sketch, E. Watts Cushman, is one of Hamilton's practicing lawyers. He was born in the south part of the

Residence of E. W. Cushman.

township, and removed with his parents to the village in early boyhood ; was educated at the public schools in the village and for the bar in the office of the Hon. Joseph Mason, whose partner he was for several years subsequent to his admission to practice. He is now in the prime of life, and is engaged in an active and lucrative business, and has the confidence of a growing clientage. He is a republican in politics, and takes an active interest in party affairs, but has never held office. In the congressional convention of 1894, in his district, comprising the counties of Madison and Onondaga, he had the unanimous support of his county for member of congress, but was beaten in the convention. His residence, at corner of Broad and Pleasant streets, is also the subject of illustration.

THE HAMILTON REPUBLICAN

F. M. Elliott.

The Hamilton Republican was founded by General Nathaniel King, and first appeared as *The Madison Farmer* in 1828. Under six changes of name and twelve proprietorships it has been continued until at the present time it is nearing the close of its 67th volume. It was as proprietor of this paper that the late G. R. Waldron commenced his more than half of a century of editorial work. While proprietor of this paper the energetic John Atwood made himself the recognized leader in Madison county journalism. Ex-Postmaster General Thomas L. James commenced his distinguished career as a proprietor and editor of the *Republican*, and during his seven years' connection with it he displayed that ability which subsequently commanded world-wide recognition. E. D. Van Slyck and others have conducted the paper with marked energy and ability. The present proprietors are W. S. Hawkins of the Waterville *Times* and F. M. Elliott of Hamilton. The last named gentleman has the management of the business, and brings to his task a knowledge gleaned from an experience of 15 years in newspaper and job office work. Under his management the paper has been enlarged to a four page thirty-six column journal, with a large and rapidly increasing circulation. The office is ocated in the Exchange Building, on Lebanon street, where it has been located during the greater part of its existence; it occupies two stories and the basement of the eastern portion of those buildings. The plant was recently pronounced by a leading dealer in printers' supplies to be one of the very largest in this portion of the state, outside of the cities. It embraces everything necessary for the complete equipment of a first class newspaper office, and also all material and facilities required for the transacting of the exceptionally large job business done by this firm. All machinery in this model office is operated by steam power. A large force of competent operatives is constantly employed, and rethan, [illegible] turned out.

J. E. ROGERS
Grocery, Meat Market and Livery Stable

A house engaged in the grocery and provision trade in Hamilton and well worthy of notice is that of Mr. J. E. Rogers, dealer in choice family groceries and meats. The establishment has an

excellent reputation for the superior quality of goods and fair, straightforward business management. Mr. Rogers has been a resident of Hamilton for the past six years. He embarked in business in 1888 and occupied a foremost position among the similar concerns here. The house since its organization has been uniformly successful, a reputation of the highest character having been sustained. In addition to his grocery and meat business, Mr. Rogers also operates a livery stable, which is well equipped for the purpose. He has on hand, at all times a number of good horses, and furnishes for all occasions conveyances in charge of competent drivers. Mr. Rogers occupies prominent positions in fraternal circles. He is an experienced and capable business man, and has a host of friends throughout this village and vicinity.

G. W. Jackson.

www.ingramcontent.com/pod-product-compliance
Lightning Source LLC
Chambersburg PA
CBHW020148170426
43199CB00010B/938